LEARN TO COOK
WITH
Nita Mehta

LEARN To COOK
With
Nita Mehta

LEARN TO COOK

With

Nita Mehta

Nita Mehta

B.Sc. (Home Science), M.Sc. (Food and Nutrition), Gold Medalist

Tanya Mehta

SNAB
Publishers Pvt. Ltd.

LEARN To COOK
with
Nita Mehta

First Hardbound Edition 2004

ISBN 81-7869-077-2   **SNAB**

Food Styling & Photography:

Layout and laser typesetting:

National Information
Technology Academy
3A/3, Asaf Ali Road
New Delhi-110002

☎ 23252948

SNAB
Publishers Pvt Ltd
3A/3 Asaf Ali Road
New   Delhi-110002
Tel:. 23250091, 23252948
Fax:. 91-11-23250091

Editorial and Marketing office:
E-159, Greater Kailash-II, N.Delhi-48
Tel: 91-11-29214011, 29218727, 29218574
Fax: 29225218
E-Mail: nitamehta@email.com
            snab@snabindia.com

The Best of *Website:*http://www.nitamehta.com
Cookery
Books *Website:* http://www.snabindia.com

Printed at:

INTERNATIONAL PRINT-O-PAC LTD

Distributed by:

THE VARIETY BOOK DEPOT
A.V.G. Bhavan, M 3 Con Circus
New Delhi - 110 001
Tel: 23417175, 23412567; Fax: 23415335
E-mail: varietybookdepot@rediffmail.com

Price: Rs. 299/-

Introduction

Here is a friend! A friend you can trust, a friend you can turn to for advice and inspiration whenever you like. I would be happy if this book made you feel that you are not alone in your kitchen, and that cooking is a rewarding experience. 'Learn to Cook' not only teaches you how to cook the most delicious food with the least bit of effort but also helps you present the food attractively. There is great information on entertaining in style and table setting for a sit down meal as well as a buffet party.

With career taking the front seat, cooking is pushed behind in many households. The children barely get time to learn cooking from the mother. And when they have to manage on their own, it seems quite difficult and sometimes rather impossible. Not to worry, the tips and the difficulties I faced as a beginner and the FAQS (frequently asked questions) by my students during my cookery sessions, have all been penned down to make cooking a pleasure. Every recipe is illustrated and the tinted boxes with recipes carry ideas and suggestions which should give you the confidence. The list of ingredients is short so that you are not tired by the time you collect all the ingredients for a recipe and then the actual cooking is pushed to the next day!

The basics of cooking which include the selection of utensils and ingredients will get you started smoothly. By giving pictures, the book makes you familiar with various spices, herbs, pulses, various meat/poultry/fish cuts and many other ingredients used in cooking. With a thorough knowledge of these, you can turn a simple vegetable/meat into something which your family and friends will love to have over and over again. The step by step illustrations and the simple way in which the recipes are worded, leave no margin for error while cooking. The chapter on "How to buy and store vegetables/meat" will help you with your grocery shopping. What's left? Common cutting techniques such as dicing, slicing, shredding and decorative cuttings too, will show new cooks how to cook with confidence.

This practical and comprehensive book is a boon for both new and experienced cooks. There are innovative and colourful fruit and vegetable garnishes which will add that finishing touch that separates a mundane meal from a spectacular one. Try the delicious recipes and get compliments galore.

Nita Mehta

ABOUT THE RECIPES

1 cup = 1 teacup which holds 200 ml water or any other liquid
1 tsp = 1 teaspoon (level)
1 tbsp = 1 tablespoon (level)
1 tbsp = 2½ tsp approx.
The recipes in this book were tested with the Indian teacup which holds 200 ml liquid.

CONTENTS

ALL ABOUT KITCHEN UTENSILS

KADHAI (wok) - The kadhai is a deep pan, round bottomed with two handles on the sides. Used mainly for frying and making Indian masala dishes. When buying one, choose a heavy bottomed one and of a medium size. Steel/Brass kadhais were used earlier, but now aluminium or non stick ones are more popular. Copper bottomed metal kadhais are also becoming popular.

PATILA (deep metal pans) - Used for boiling water, milk, rice, pasta etc. Buy a heavy bottom one. Deep non stick pots with handles are also available which are very handy for making soups, rice and curries.

PRESSURE COOKER - A must have for the Indian kitchen. It cooks the food fast by forming steam from boiling water which is put inside the cooker. A 5 litre capacity will serve the family as well as do good for the parties too. Remember to remove the rubber gasket when you clean the cooker. Once the pressure is formed, keep it on low heat to cook food. Rajmah (beans), channas (chick peas) or even pulses and lentils (dals) cook well in the pressure cooker.

NON STICK FRYING PAN (saute pan, skillet) - A pan about 2" high is ideal for shallow frying tikkis, kebabs and other snacks. It makes a good utensil for cooking dry/semi dry dishes too. The vegetables/meat lie flat in a single layer on the wide bottom making them crunchy on the outside and yet moist from inside. Remember to use a plastic or a wooden spoon/spatula to stir and fry in all nonstick vessels. Metallic ones will scratch the non stick finish and ruin it. Avoid strong detergents for washing them, warm soapy water is best. It is good to have one small (about 7" diameter) and one big (10 " diameter) pans. Dosas and pancakes too can be made conveniently in them.

Sauce Pan - These are deep pans with a handle. Useful for making tea, blanching vegetables in water or working with food where some sauce is needed. Usually these are made of stainless steel and are available in various sizes. Nonstick ones are also available.

TAWA (griddle) - A heavy iron tawa makes good chappatis. Buy one with a handle. These days non stick griddles are also available.

CHAKLA-BELAN (rolling board-rolling pin) - A marble or heavy weight rolling board is ideal for rolling out dough for chapattis, poori etc. A wooden rolling pin with it makes the set complete. Plastic rolling pins are available but I am not too comfortable with them.

PARAT (shallow bowl to knead dough) - Shallow bowl to make dough, generally stainless steel. Buy a medium size even if you are a small family, because if the bowl is too small, the surrounding area tends to get messy while making the dough. Dough can also be made in a food processor.

MIXIE (mixer-grinder) - Good to make onion paste or puree fresh tomatoes. Buy one with a heavy motor which can grind even rice or dals for dosa and pancake batter. There is generally another separate blender jar for making lassi (smoothies), shakes etc.

Coffee or Spice Grinder - This is generally available alongwith the mixer/ grinder. Available separately also. It is very handy for grinding smaller quantities. Pastes of small quantities of anything never comes out smooth in the big mixer/grinder. This small grinder is extremely useful for making ginger paste, garlic paste, cahewnut paste etc.

ELECTRIC HAND MIXER - An easy way to whip cream and beat cake batters and other dessert mixes. It can also be used to mash potatoes.

KADCCHI (laddle) - Large, long handled spoon with a small shallow bowl like spoon at the end. Should be strong enough for stirring masalas.

PALTA (pancake turner) - These broad metal turners have thin, flexible yet sturdy blade that will slide easily under the food and then be strong enough to turn the food. Not just for pancakes, it's great for turning kebabs, chicken breasts and fish fillets. Ideally choose one with a heat resistant handle.

CHHARA, PAUNI (slotted spoon) A big round, flat spoon with holes and a long handle. Serves good for removing fried food from oil as it drains out the oil nicely through the holes. Also used to lift solid foods out of cooking liquids.

TONGS - Especially good to use when grilling foods, but can also can be used to lift or turn food without piercing it. Cooking tongs should be made of metal, in contrast to salad tongs, which might be wooden or plastic & usually have a larger end for tossing a salad. Must keep one fancy pair handy for picking up snacks.

STEEL KI BIG CHHANNI (colander) A big, wide strainer with large holes for draining cooked rice, pasta and for draining fresh vegetables after washing.

WIRE WHISK OR BALLOON WHISK - Great for beating eggs & preparing batters, sauces, raitas and dressing as well as for all purpose mixing.

VEGETABLE PEELER - Much easier to use than a knife to remove a thin peel from apples, potatoes, carrots and many other fruits & vegetables.

KNIVES - A plain and a serrated one for cutting tomato slices etc. is good to possess. A big one for cutting meat is also useful.

MIXING BOWLS - Choose two or three deep bowls in different sizes. A large mixing bowl can serve as a salad bowl.

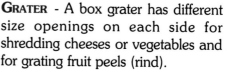

GRATER - A box grater has different size openings on each side for shredding cheeses or vegetables and for grating fruit peels (rind).

CHOPPING BOARD - It is a wooden or plastic flat plank which makes chopping faster. Wooden boards are good but for chopping meat plastic boards are better. Wash them immediately after cutting raw meat, poultry or fish.

STRAINER/SIEVE - A small one for straining tea is a must. Have a big one for draining the liquid off cooked foods, straining tamarind pulp or sifting flour.

CAN OPENER - Very useful for opening tins of pineapple, corn and other canned foods. Purchase one that's easy to wash after each use.

LEMON SQUEEZER - Takes out juice from lemons without the bitter seeds going in.

MELON SCOOPER - A very handy tool for decorating desserts or mocktails. Lovely fruit balls of 2 different sizes can be made from any soft fruit like mangoes, papaya, water melon etc. It is also useful for scooping potatoes or cucumber for filling.

KITCHEN SCISSORS - A very handy tool for cutting milk packets or for cutting the tetrapacks of other foods like tomato puree, cream etc.

MOOSAL (pestle & mortar) - A deep bowl with a sturdy base with a compatible thick rod like pestle is used for grinding tiny, hard seeds and spices such as fennel (saunf), cardamom seeds (illaichi) other spices like cloves (laung) etc. Even used for crushing garlic flakes. It can be made of brass, steel, porcelain or even wood. The end of the pestle and the inside bottom surface of the bowl should be slightly rough for maximum friction.

PRESENTING & GARNISHING FOOD

Serving tasty food in an unappetizing manner is not the way of life today. The food needs to look pleasing to the eye too. With just a little effort, your food will make a fabulous first impression. Remember, the garnish is the finishing touch, so add it right before serving. Here are a few ideas to get you started:

Float slices of lemons, oranges, fresh or tinned cherries in a glass of lemonade or iced tea or any drink. If the slices of orange are big, cut them into half. And remember to slice the orange along with the peel. The peel adds a tang to the drink.

Cut a small slit in a strawberry and insert it on the rim of the glass. The cut made is very small and the fruit is pushed on the rim, so that it stays there firmly. Never make the cut too long and never use a tinned fruit as it is soft and it might fall off.

Serve your hari chutney, salsa, mayonnaise or cheese dip in cabbage or capsicum cups instead of the usual glass bowls. For a good rounded cup of cabbage, cut the cabbage leaf from the stalk end. Pull gently from the cut end to get a nice rounded cup. Dip in a bowl filled with cold water and keep in the fridge till serving time to get a crisp cabbage cup.

For capsicum cups, take a green or coloured capsicum, slice off the top and scoop out. Cut the edge into 'VV' with a small kitchen scissors. Place these cups filled with the dip or sauce, in the snack platter.

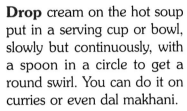

Drop cream on the hot soup put in a serving cup or bowl, slowly but continuously, with a spoon in a circle to get a round swirl. You can do it on curries or even dal makhani.

Float paper thin slices of carrot or cucumber in a soup bowl. If the cucumber is large, cut the slice into half. Do not peel the cucumber. Another way of serving is to drop ½ tsp of finely chopped carrot or capsicum in each cup of soup at the time of serving, for the desired crunch.

When the snack cannot be garnished as in rolls, cutlets, pakoras etc. remember to decorate the platter in which they are served. **Arrange** lettuce or sprigs of parsley or mint on snack platters or trays. Remember to submerge the greens in chilled water and keep in the fridge for 2-3 hours to become crisp.

Chocolate Vermicelli or Sprinklers: Sprinkle 1 tsp of these at serving time on the top of a dessert or cake or on whipped cream. You can also grate chocolate instead of sprinklers. To get good flakes of chocolate, the chocolate should never be too cold. Remove from fridge and grate after a while when it is no longer too cold.

Mint Leaves: These add colour to food. Keep leaves in cold water for 2-3 hours to get crisp green leaves and arrange a sprig of leaves on the dessert or a baked Continental dish.

Crushed Cookies: Coarsely crush cookies or biscuits like chocolate chip or good-day biscuits with a rolling pin, and sprinkle on half the portion of a dessert. Also a border of crushed cookies instead of a border of whipped cream looks more tempting to the health conscious people of today. Use chocolate cookies on a light coloured surface and vice-versa.

Marble Effect: Mix some chocolate sauce or jam or fruit crush lightly into your dessert mixture or cream to get a marble effect.

Fascinating Forks: Place 2 forks on any dessert crossing each other. Sprinkle cocoa all over from a sieve. Pick up the forks to get a beautiful design.

Chocolate thins & nutties: Chocolate thins are imported paper thin squares of chocolate available in a box. Cut a chocolate thin diagonally into 2 pieces to get 2 triangular pieces. These triangles stand beautifully in the centre of a chocolate dessert. Arrange these halves on a dollop of cream topped with a cherry. You can also arrange just 3 nutties in the centre of a dessert and top with a sprig of mint.

Decorating the dessert plate: Put 4-5 drops of chocolate sauce in a circular row. Put drops of another sauce like strawberry sauce or crush next to the chocolate drop. Run a knife through the drops to create a feather effect.

To serve snacks: like rolls or kebabs, pour some tomato ketchup or hari chutney across the rolls with a spoon or dot the kebab or balls with it. Choose a slightly bigger platter and place a fresh sprig of mint or parsley or coriander in the serving platter next to the rolls.

SIMPLE DECORATIVE VEGETABLE CARVING

CARROT FLOWERS: *If the dish requires round slices of carrots, cut the carrot into round flowers instead. It enhances the look of stir fried dishes. These flowers are usually seen in Chinese dishes but they look good in Indian mixed vegetables too.*

For carrot flowers, peel a thick, big carrot. Cut into two pieces to get 2 shorter lengths. Firmly holding the carrot upright, with a small sharp knife, make 1/8 inch broad and deep lengthwise cuts along the length of the carrot. Tilt the knife slightly to take out the thin long piece from the cut to get a groove. Make 2-3 more grooves leaving equal space between them. Carefully, cut the carrot into round slices.

SPRING ONION FLOWERS: *Go well with tandoori snacks or in Chinese dishes.*

To make spring onion flowers, cut off about ¼ inch piece from the white bulb end and leaving 3" from the bulb, cut off the greens. Slice the bulb thinly lengthwise till the end of the bulb. Now make similar cuts at right angles. Similarly for a green side, cut the green leaves with a pair of scissors, almost till the stem end to get thin strips. Place in iced water for some time until it opens up like a flower.

CARROT & RADISH TUBEROSES: *These look great when placed on the side of a salad, or next to the snacks on the serving platter. A sprig of green leaves of coriander, mint or parsley placed next to the flowers make them look prettier.*

Take a slender carrot or radish. Peel and wash it. Make a sharp angled cut, at about a height of 1½", about ½" downwards and inwards. Make 2 similar cuts from the remaining sides - all the cuts should meet at the end. Hold the top of the carrot with one hand, and the base with the other. Twist the lower portion to break off the top portion. You will have a tuberose in one hand and the remaining part of the carrot in the other. Trim the left over carrot to get a pointed end. Make more flowers from the left over carrot. Keep them in ice-cold water for upto 3-4 days without getting spoilt. You can make such flowers with white radish (mooli) also.

LEMON TWIST: *Looks good on a lemon dessert or on channas or a rice dish. Small orange twists too look good.*

Cut a fresh, big and firm lemon into half. Cut a slice from any one piece. Keeping the slice flat on the board, cut halfway from any side of the slice till almost the centre. Holding the slice upright, gently twist the two cut ends in opposite directions to get a twist.

TOMATO ROSE: *A very useful garnish. Do it on salads, snack platters, rice dishes or any stir fried dishes.*

Take a very firm and red tomato. Beginning at the stem end, start cutting the skin as though you were peeling it in a long strip. The strip should be as long as possible, as thin as possible and about ½" to 1" wide. See that you keep changing the width of the strip as you go on peeling it. Do not let the strip be uniform in width. The rose looks more natural if the strip is cut uneven. If while peeling, it breaks, keep the broken part aside for use later on & continue cutting the peel.

Now start rolling up the long strip firmly. Place the other parts of the strip around the rolled peel.

The tomato strip should now look like a real rose.

CHILLI FLOWER: *A chilli flower made from fresh red or green chilli is a wonderful garnish for a spicy dish.*

Choose a slightly thick chilli. Cut into half starting from the tip almost till the end, leaving ½" from the stem end. Cut each half with a scissor into many thin strips, keeping all intact at the base. Put the chilli in chilled water for 4-5 hours in the fridge. It opens up to a flower.

TOMATO BUTTERFLIES: *Goes well with tandoori snacks.*
Cut a firm, longish tomato into 4 long pieces. Holding a piece with pulp side down, from the tip start to cut the skin a little more than halfway. Keep the tomato piece upright with the tip down and the peeled skin away from the pulpy portion, to get a curve on the separated tomato skin.

COLOURED CAPSICUM BASKETS: Slice the top of a coloured (yellow, red or green capsicum). Make a ½" deep V cuts all around the edge to get a 'VVVV' edge. Leave the bunch of seeds in it as they are. Place on the side of a large platter of salad.

All garnishes should be made a day or two, before the party and kept in the fridge dipped in chilled water in a bowl. You will hardly get enough time on the party day.

Fruit Balls: Use a melon scooper to make balls of water melon or mango or papaya and arrange on top of a dessert in a heap.

Frosted Fruits: Dip fruits like grapes in lemon juice and roll in powdered sugar. You can also simply sprinkle some powdered sugar through a sieve on the arranged fruits.

Fruit Fans: Slice a large grape or a strawberry lengthwise into thin slices, cutting almost till the end, but keep the end part of the fruit together. Fan out the slices by pushing the slices gently towards your right, so that they open up like a fan. Place on a dessert or salad.

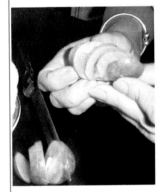

Fruit Bowls for Salads

To make fruit bowls: Make a deep 'V' cut in the centre of the watermelon. To do this, make about 2" slant cut first and then another one a little away from the first one, but which meets at the bottom. Continue cutting in the same way all around the water melon to get a VVVV edge when the two pieces are separated. When cutting, keep the knife tilted and go deep inside. Separate the two pieces. Make the piece hollow, keeping a little red border showing. Cover the empty bowl with a plastic wrap and refrigerate. Fill salad in it at serving time. You may add some chopped watermelon pieces to the salad.

Fruity Sticks: These look great on rice biryani or on the side of a snack platter or when placed on the mouth of a narrow mocktail glass.
4 black grapes, 4 cherries or small strawberries, 1 lemon - cut into 8 pieces, 4-6 large mint leaves (dipped in water for 2-3 hours or more), few tooth picks. Thread cherry or a strawberry, a mint leaf, a grape and finally a lemon piece on a tooth pick.

BRINJAL (Baingan)

Round big variety ... Dark, firm, smooth and shiny looks handsome. The lighter one in weight is preferred over a heavy one for the same size, as the heavy one generally has more seeds. The smaller variety is easier to choose. See that they are smooth and blemish free.

What makes brinjals bitter?

When they get too big with too many seeds and too old with a wrinkly skin and soft flesh- the taste is slightly bitter. Choose smaller ones!

BROCCOLI (Hari Gobhi)

Buy fresh, tight, dark green heads that are not blooming and with no wilt or yellowing. Avoid woody or hollow stalks. Keep in the refrigerator for 2-3 days.

BABY CORN (Chhoti Makai)

Buy ones which are not more than 3-4" long as they mature when the grow in size. Choose, thin, slender ones. The cob is tasty and slender and is edible along with the kernels unlike the regular corn where only the kernels are edible. Store baby corns in ziplock/plastic bags in the refrigerator for 4-5 days.

CAULIFLOWER (Phool Gobhi)

Buy a clean white one, with no black spots. Avoid woody or hollow stalks. Keep it in the fridge, without removing the outer green leaves for a week or 10 days.

Don't buy this cauliflower!

Try separating a few florets on the head to check if it has any insects. Green, slimmy ones may be present. Don't pick it up.

CABBAGE (Patta Gobhi)

Choose a firm, round one with a tight head and with dark green outer leaves attached. Make sure that there are no brown spots or cracked leaves. Many shop keepers trim the outer green leaves as they wilt, leaving only the pale inner head exposed. Usable but not as tasty! Cabbage keeps well in the refrigerator for a week.

Is the lighter weight cabbage better because it is cheaper for the same size?

No, a cabbage which is heavy and solid for its size is definitely better.

CAPSICUMS (Simla Mirch)

Green ones are more commonly used. Medium size with a bright green colour are good. Check for decay at the stem end. Now coloured ones are available too and are sweeter in taste than the green ones.

CARROTS (Gajar)

Select long, slender, young carrots - firm and smooth, not lumpy or withered. Store carrots in the refrigerator for a week or 10 days.

Corn (Bhutta)

ook for ears with moist, grassy green, tightly wrapped husks with just a bit of dry, rown tassel peeking from the tips. Feel on the outside of the husk, all the way up to ne tip. It should feel full and firm. If your vegetable waala (vendor) allows, peel a bit f the husk back and look for decay or worms and make certain that the kernels are lump and evenly spaced. Pierce one kernel with a fingernail, and a fresh corn will quirt a milky juice. No juice? The corn is not to be bought.

o *store corn* -- Try not to store for more than 2 days. The sugar changes to starch, making it taste not as good s before. Put them unhusked in a plastic bag in the fridge.

Colocassia (Arbi)

Buy pieces which are medium size, about 2" long and slightly thick and plump with thin skin. Buy pieces without knots. Stores well for a week in the refrigerator. You can store it outside too, but it gets dry faster and tastes waxy when cooked.

Ginger (Adrak)

Buy pieces which are firm and plump. The skin should be thin, light brown with a slight heen. Do not buy a piece with lots of shoots or knobs coming out of the main piece. This nakes it difficult to peel. Keep in the fridge for 2 weeks. The left over used portion can be kept in a zip lock/plastic bag and kept in the fridge to prevent it from drying out.

Grating a mature piece of ginger!

This will give you a fibrous mass, therefore chop it finely or grind in a mixer to a paste. Do not buy ginger which is very mature. A mature ginger has a thick skin and holes and feels very hard and dry.

Garlic (Lahasun)

There are small and big sized garlic pods. The small garlic pods have more intense flavour. Store garlic in a dark, well ventilated place (outside the fridge) and they should last upto 2 months.

Big or small pods of garlic?

Though the small ones are more flavourful, but sometimes they become difficult to peel. If you have no help, go or the big sized ones and use a little extra in the dish.

Gourds or Squash (Tinda, Tori, Lauki)

Buy gourds with unbruised, firm and glossy skins. Keep in the refrigerator for 4-5 days. The smaller sized ones are better. The mature, fibrous ones get a hint of yellow. The skin or peel when pricked with the fingernail does not resist the nail too hard.

Pale green or dark green colour - what is better in green vegetables?

The greener the vegetable, the more nutritious it is. Dark green is definitely better.

GREEN BEANS (Phalli)

Also known as French beans. Buy small, slender, green ones for sweetness. Snap the end to see if they are tender. If they don't break off, they are a little tough and not too good. They are best when they are crisp. Store them in the refrigerator for 3-4 days. These have strings, snip off the stem ends and zip off the string.

GREEN CHILLIES (Hari Mirch)

The smaller the chilli, the hotter it is. Store them in a zip lock in the fridge for a week. I generally like to deseed the chilli while cooking, to reduce the heat.

KARELA (Bitter gourd)

The greener and the more slender it is, the better. As the vegetable matures, it acquires a hint of yellow. It should be firm and not spongy to touch. The overmature ones have big, thick seeds whereas the tender ones have thin, flat seeds. If the seeds are big, remove them before cooking.

LOTUS STEM (Bhein/Kamal kakri)

Firm, plump and white stems are great. These have holes which can collect a lot of grit and mud and give you a tough time cleaning them. (You can use a tooth pick if you do fall into the trap of the vegetable vendor!) To avoid this, choose ones which have closed ends, which stop the dirt from getting inside.

MUSHROOMS (Khumb)

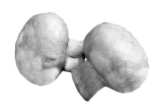

Fresh mushrooms are very tight, very firm and very white - meaning you will not be able to see the gills underneath the cap. As the mushroom loses its moisture, the cap shrinks, exposing the gills. The mushroom becomes flabby, and the surface gets slimy. Purchase your mushrooms no more than 1-2 days before using them since they are highly perishable. Store in a loose paper bag or in a container with air-holes in it. They will sweat and get slimy if they are kept too tightly wrapped. Dry mushrooms are also available.

Never use wild mushrooms. It can be a life threatening activity.

OKRA/LADY'S FINGER (Bhindi)

Buy small size ones, about 2-3" long, and firm. The larger ones tend to be fibrous. Store them in a plastic bag for not more than 2-3 days, since they start to turn brown at the edges after that.

Break the pointed tip of an okra. If the tip snaps off easily, the okra is fresh and tender.

SPINACH/ (Palak) MUSTARD GREENS (Sarson ka Saag)

Choose a bunch with fresh and green leaves with tender stems. Avoid leaves with a slimmy sign of decay. Although greens are best when used quickly, they can be stored, unwashed and wrapped in paper towels, in a plastic bag for 2-3 days.

How to pick up the best bundle of spinach?

The smaller the leaves, the better they taste.

ONIONS (Pyaz)

Choose medium size, firm, heavy, unblemished onions with dry, papery skins. Avoid damp, bruised, sprouting soft onions or those with black mold. These store well in a dark ventilated place, (outside the fridge) and they should last upto 2-3 weeks. Humidity in the kitchen will encourage decay.

PEAS (Matar)

Firm, green and full pods are best. Do not buy very thin or flat pea pods as you might feel cheated once you open them at home. Peas are highly perishable since their high sugar content begins to turn to starch from the moment they are picked. So you can keep the peas in the fridge for a week, but the taste is no longer sweet and too good. Of course they can be used!

POTATOES (Aloo)

Buy firm, heavy, unblemished ones without spongy spots or sprouted "eyes", or those that are shrivelled or cracked. Store potatoes for about 10 days, away from light, but in a well ventilated place, but not in the refrigerator. Refrigeration converts the starch to sugar and gives the potatoes an "off" taste.

In storage at home, some potatoes will begin to sprout- use or discard?

As long as the potato is still firm and not soft or wrinkled it is okay. Just cut out the sprouts and cook the rest.

Do the green portions in potatoes make them useless?

Some times, there is a green tinge under the potato skin. Cut the green parts away, the remaining sections are okay.

TOMATOES (Tamatar)

Choose medium, firm red tomatoes. The bright red colour is important or your dish will not have a pleasant red colour. Store them in the fridge for a week.

Buy larger quantities of onions, potatoes, garlic, ginger and tomatoes, always enough to last a week or so, as they are used very frequently in cooking and do not perish easily if stored carefully.

Vegetables should be washed very well before cutting to remove dirt and the pesticides sprinkled on them.

Chopping: to cut into small pieces

The vegetable is cut into small pieces. Holding on to the vegetable firmly, cut the vegetable lengthwise into slices and then holding on firmly, give the sliced vegetable a quick turn at a right angle. Now cut the sliced vegetable again into slices which will result in finely chopped pieces. Onions and tomatoes are usually chopped in the recipes.

Shredding: to cut into thin, long pieces

The vegetables are cut into thin, strips or shreds. Spinach, lettuce, cabbage are all shredded. Carrot can be grated on the big holes of a grater to get shredded carrot.

Dicing: to cut into very small cubes

The vegetables are cut into dice or small cubes. The vegetables are first cut lengthwise into ¼ or ½ inch thick strips/fingers and several such strips/fingers are kept together and further cut into ¼ inch pieces.

Slicing: to cut completely through the vegetable to get slices

The vegetables are cut into thin slices. The thickness depends on what is specified in each individual recipe. Tomatoes, carrots, mushrooms, onions etc. are sliced in quite a few recipes.

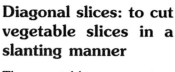

Diagonal slices: to cut vegetable slices in a slanting manner

The vegetables are cut into thin slices in a slanting manner in such a way that there are more exposed surfaces. Vegetables such as asparagus, carrots, celery or French beans are usually diagonally sliced.

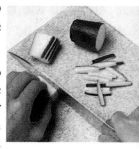

Jullienes: to cut into thin match stick like pieces

The vegetables are cut into thin slices lengthwise. The slices are stacked together and cut lengthwise to get thin match sticks. Carrots and cucumber jullienes look good.

Rings and Half Rings: to cut vegetables widthwise into rounds

Vegetables like onions or capsicums are cut widthwise to get rounds. The onion slices are then separated to give full rings. For half rings, cut the vegetables first into half and then cut widthwise to get half rings. When opened the half rings look like thin strips of onion and can be used as shredded onion also.

Florets of Cauliflower

Remove the extra stalk, leaving about ½" stalk near the base of the head. Cut the flower into two halves, right through the stalk. Break into pieces as the recipe demands.

Deseed a green chilli

Cut the green chilli into half lengthwise Scrape away the seeds from both pieces and then chop or use as required.

Removing seeds from capsicums

Cut into half lengthwise and again into half lengthwise. Cut the white portion and discard. Proceed as required.

How to cut leafy greens?

For greens like spinach (paalak) or fenugreek (methi), remove discoloured and slimy leaves. Wash leaves in several changes of water. Hold a small bunch on the chopping board, then holding the bunch tightly, cut off the hard stems and then start cutting the leaves finely.

How to get tomato pieces without pulp?

Cut a firm tomato into 4 pieces lengthwise. Remove pulp from each piece. Now cut the big piece into smaller pieces or strips.

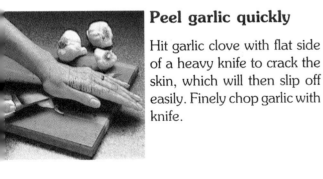

Peel garlic quickly

Hit garlic clove with flat side of a heavy knife to crack the skin, which will then slip off easily. Finely chop garlic with knife.

Right way to cut cabbage

Cut into half first and then again into half. Keeping the cut side, flat on a board, chop or cut into thin long pieces.

	ENGLISH NAME			HINDI NAME
1	Sesame Seeds		1	Til
2	Mustard Seeds		2	Rai, Sarson
3	Melon Seeds		3	Magaz
4	Coriander Seeds		4	Saboot dhania
5	Coriander Seeds, Ground		5	Dhania powder
6	Mango Powder		6	Amchoor
7	Red Chilli Powder		7	Lal Mirch
8	Cumin Seeds, White		8	Jeera
9	Carom Seeds		9	Ajwain
10	Fennel		10	Saunf
11	Cumin Seeds, Black		11	Shah Jeera
12	Garam Masala - A Spice Blend		12	Garam Masala
13	Asafoetida		13	Hing
14	Saffron		14	Kesar
15	Fenugreek Leaves, Dried		15	Kasoori methi
16	Fenugreek Seeds		16	Methi dana
17	Pomegranate Seeds, Dried		17	Anardana
18	Nigella Seeds		18	Kalaunji
19	Turmeric		19	Haldi
20	Cloves		20	Laung
21	Nutmeg		21	Jaiphal
22	Peppercorns		22	Saboot kali mirch
23 24	Cardamom Pods		23 24	Elaichi
25	Mace		25	Javitri
26	Cinnamon		26	Dalchini
27	Fresh Green Chillies		27	Hari mirch
28	Red Chillies, Dried		28	Sukhi lal mirch
29	Ginger		29	Adrak
30	Garlic		30	Lahsun
31	Coriander, Fresh		31	Hara dhania
32	Bay Leaves		32	Tej patta
33	Curry Leaves		33	Kari patta
34	Mint		34	Poodina

Did You Know?

Spices are the seeds or bark of the plants where as Herbs are the leafy parts and stem of the plant, so coriander seed is a spice whereas coriander leaf is a herb.

SPICES

ASAFOETIDA (Hing)

This pungent, almost unpleasant smelling spice is used in very small amounts in a dish and sauteed in oil before adding the other ingredients. It imparts a pleasant flavour to the cooked dish and also aids digestion.

CAROM SEEDS (Ajwain)

These are tiny brown seeds which are slightly pungent. When crushed, they release a strong and lightly aromatic, thyme like fragrance, but on cooking the flavour becomes milder.

CARDAMOM PODS (Ilaichi)

The pods can be used whole or the husk can be removed to release the seeds. These have a sharp initial bite that soon mellows into a delicate and refreshing fragrance.

There are two types of cardamom pods available, the small green (chhoti or hari ilaichi) and the larger black ones (bari or moti ilaichi).

CINNAMON (Dalchini)

The true cinnamon has tightly rolled tubular sticks. The Indian cinnamon has thicker flattish sticks. Cinnamon has a delicate, sweet aroma.

CORIANDER SEEDS (Saboot dhaniya)

These are small, ribbed and spherical seeds. When lightly roasted and crushed, these add a wonderful flavour to the cooked dishes.

CUMIN SEEDS, (Jeera)

These are slender, oval seeds. The commonly used variety is pale in colour and generally referred as cumin seeds. There is another darker variety which is not so common called black cumin (shah jeera). These are used for flavouring curries and rice.

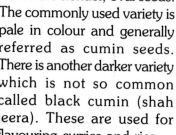

CLOVES (Laung)

These dried unopened flower buds have a sharp pungent and almost bitter taste.

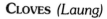

FENNEL (Saunf)

These oval, greenish seeds have a sweetish taste and are used to flavour rice dishes (biryanis), curries and pickles.

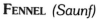

FENUGREEK SEEDS (Methi dana)

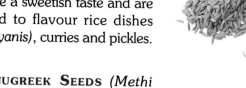

These are flat, oblong, mustard brownish seeds. Although these have a slight bitter taste, when raw, but when cooked right, enhance the flavour greatly in vegetables and curries. Always use them in small amounts in a dish.

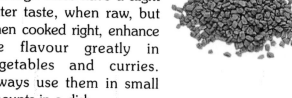

MACE (Javitri)

This is the lacy covering of the seed of the nutmeg tree. It has a rich, warm fragrance and a sweet flavour. Use it very sparingly, adding it to only rich and creamy dishes. Mostly it is added to various spice blends.

MELON SEEDS (Magaz)

These are white, egg-shaped, shelled seeds of melons. It makes the Indian curries thick, rich and flavourful. It is also added to drinks and desserts.

MUSTARD SEEDS (Rai, Sarson)

These may be small reddish brown (rai) or slighter bigger blackish (sarson) seeds. They have a sharp, pungent flavour which mellows after they are cooked in hot oil or dry roasted. The Southern part of India uses mustard to flavour almost all their dishes.

NIGELLA SEEDS (Kalaunji)

These are charcoal black triangular seeds, resembling onion seeds, and are often mistakenly referred to as such. Nigella seeds have a mild flavour, like oregano, which enhances when added to baked flat breads (naan and roti). Also used in pickles.

NUTMEG (Jaiphal)

It is the oval, brown kernel of the seed of the nutmeg tree. It has a rich warm fragrance and a sweet antiseptic flavour. It is generally grated and just a pinch is added to dishes.

POPPY SEEDS (Khus-Khus)

These are very tiny, beige coloured seeds which have a nutty aroma. It is often used to give texture to Indian dishes. They are also sprinkled over naan or breads before being cooked in the oven. There is a dark grey European variety, but in India the light ivory coloured ones are more popular. These should be stored in the fridge as they turn rancid and acquire an off taste when kept in a warm place.

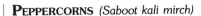

PEPPERCORNS (Saboot kali mirch)

Ground or crushed black peppercorns add a delectable taste to soups, salads and main dishes. These are even used whole in the preparation of vegetables and rice dishes like pullaos.

RED CHILLIES, DRIED

These keep well in an air-tight container in a cool, dry place, for 6-8 months. These can be used whole or dry roasted in a pan and crushed in a spice grinder to give you red chilli flakes. Before crushing, break into pieces and discard some of the seeds to reduce the heat.

STAR ANISE (Chakri Phool)

The dried, hard, brown, star shaped fruit which has a fennel flavour. It is an important ingredient used in the Chinese five spice powder and also in Kashmiri cuisine.

SAFFRON (Kesar)

It imparts a strong yellow colour. Only a pinch is needed to impart a unique penetrating taste. To get the maximum flavour and colour, soak a few threads into some very hot liquid for atleast 15 minutes and then add the golden liquid along with the threads to the dish.

SESAME SEEDS (Til)

These small, teardrop-shaped, flat seeds are quite tasteless in their raw state but impart a wonderful nutty flavour after roasting. These range from cream to black in colour. The taste and visual appeal of baked or fried food is greatly enhanced, when they are coated with sesame seeds.

THE INDIAN SPICE BOX

Mostly every Indian kitchen will have this box with various compartments to hold the basic spices and salt.

- **CORIANDER SEEDS, GROUND** *(Dhaniya powder)*: Coriander seeds are ground to a fine powder. This is an important constituent of most curries. It helps in thickening curries.

- **CUMIN SEEDS, WHITE** *(Jeera):* These are one of the most important spice seeds in cooking. These are pale brown, oval seeds which have a strong aroma. When added to hot oil, they turn more fragrant. These can be used whole or ground. Sometimes the cumin seeds are dry roasted on a tawa (griddle) till they turn brownish and very aromatic. The roasted seeds when ground, lend a delicious flavour to yogurt or raitas.

- **GARAM MASALA:** A mixture of spices which can be made by grinding whole spices in a coffee/spice grinder, or purchased ready-made from grocery stores. A typical mixture includes cumin seeds, peppercorns, cloves, cinnamon and black cardamom seeds. The recipe for home made garam masala follows later.

- **MANGO POWDER** *(Amchoor):* Raw mangoes are sun dried and ground to a fine powder. It is used as a souring agent instead of lime or lemon juice in cooked dishes.

- **RED CHILLI POWDER** *(Lal mirch):* This fiery ground spice should be used with caution. The heat varies from brand to brand, so adjust quantities to suit your taste buds. Paprika or degi mirch may be substituted if you do not want the dish to be too hot.

- **TURMERIC** *(Haldi):* This bright yellow, bitter tasting spice is sold ground. It is used mainly for colour rather than flavour. It has great antiseptic properties too.

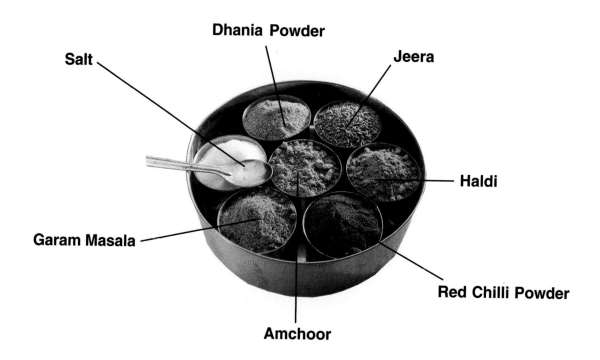

Never add a spice to very hot oil. It will burn and lose its aroma. On the other hand, if a spice is added to oil which is not hot at all, it does not bring out its full aroma. So always heat oil and then reduce heat before you throw the spice in the oil.

MINT *(Poodina):*

Only the leaves are used. It is available in dried form also. Goes well in yogurt dishes or as a garnish on mocktails or desserts.

CORIANDER/CILANTRO *(Hara dhaniya):*

The green stalks are full of flavour and so the stalks should also be finely chopped along with the leaves and used in flavouring dishes. Makes a good garnish too.

CURRY LEAVES *(Kari patta):*

These are used mostly in South Indian cooking. They are available fresh or dried. Most Indian homes grow a young plant in a pot, so as to get maximum flavour from the fresh leaves. Used abundantly in South-Indian cooking.

BAY LEAVES *(Tej patta):*

These fragrant leaves with pointed ends are used in their dried form. These are used in curries and rice preparations.

FENUGREEK GREENS, DRIED *(Kasoori methi):*

The fresh greens of the fenugreek plant are dried and used to flavour both, curries and dry dishes.

OREGANO: Also known as wild marjoram, it is available in two forms - fresh and dried. Dried oregano is very concentrated and stronger in flavour and should be used sparingly. It combines very well in Italian cooking in pasta and pizza sauces, especially tomato based dishes.

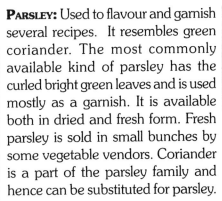

PARSLEY: Used to flavour and garnish several recipes. It resembles green coriander. The most commonly available kind of parsley has the curled bright green leaves and is used mostly as a garnish. It is available both in dried and fresh form. Fresh parsley is sold in small bunches by some vegetable vendors. Coriander is a part of the parsley family and hence can be substituted for parsley.

THYME: A herb which belongs to the mint family. The leaves are used in fresh or dry form. It is highly aromatic and should therefore be used sparingly. Leaves of carom (ajwain) can be used as substitute for thyme.

BASIL: It belongs to the 'tulsi' family. It is available in dried form or as fresh basil leaves which are packed and sold by some vegetable vendors. Dried herbs are more concentrated so substitute 1 -2 tsp for ¼ cup of fresh basil leaves. The young, tender leaves of tulsi which is called the Holy basil, can be substituted for this sweet basil, but since they are much stronger than the real sweet basil, the leaves of this holy basil should be used sparingly in the recipe.

What is the best way to store basil and mint?

Once I put basil leaves in a bowl of water thinking they would remain fresh and green. To my disappointment, they turned black! Then I discovered that standing basil in a glass of water with the leaves above the water, kept them fresh and green for a few days. During winters, you can keep this pretty bouquet on the kitchen counter and in summers keep the herbs in the glass in the fridge.

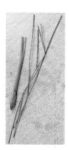

LEMON GRASS:

It is a common ingredient in Thai cuisine. The flavour of lemon grass is similar to that of lemon, yet it has its very own unique and haunting piquancy. To use, discard the bottom 1" of the stalk and peel some of the outer leaves. Chop the stalk and use it in curry pastes. The upper grass like portion is not edible and so it is added to dishes like soups, rice and curries to flavour them but removed from the dish before serving. Lemon grass will keep well for about 1-2 weeks in the fridge. Use 1-2 stalks per dish.

In its absence, lemon rind makes a good substitute. To get lemon rind, grate a firm, fresh lemon on the grater without applying pressure. Grate only the yellow outer skin without grating the white pith beneath it. Rind of 2 lemons would do good for a stalk of lemon grass.

CHIVES:

These are sold in bunches. Have an onion flavour and resemble very slender green onions. Rarely cooked, they are usually snipped with a scissors and sprinkled on a finished dish, just before serving to preserve their mildness. These go very well with Continental dishes.

CELERY:

It has thick green stalks with leaves like the coriander, but much bigger in size. Only the stalks are edible. They taste great in salads and give a distinguished taste to the stock made for a soup. To use celery, discard the lower hard portion of the stalk and chop the rest of the stalk, preferably into slanting slices. The leaves can be used as a garnish.

DILL (soye):

It is mainly used for flavouring soups, sauces and many other dishes. In India it is available in plenty during the winter months. A dish of potatoes cooked with dill is a delicacy. Fresh dill has bright green hair-fine feathery leaves and makes a beautiful garnish too. It is available in its dried form too.

Fresh or Dried?

Herbs are mostly best used in their fresh form, but their dried forms are equally commonly used in the kitchen. In fact some herbs like oregano and bay leaves are used in their dried form more where as coriander and celery are used more in their fresh form.

MORE ABOUT HERBS

How do I substitute dried herb for a fresh one?

For best flavours, use fresh herbs. If some fresh herbs are not available at a given time, substitute the dried herb for it. Dried herbs have more intense flavour than fresh, so generally 1 tbsp of fresh herb for 1 tsp of dried herb is used. Crush the leaves of dried herbs between your fingers to release the flavour before adding them to the dish.

When should the herb be added to the dish during cooking to give out its full flavour?

Add herbs at the end of cooking, as heat of the food helps release their flavour. Sprinkling fresh coriander after removing the dish from fire will not release the full fragrance of coriander. It is then just a garnish. But do not add the herbs too early to the cooking dish also, as the vivid green colour of the herb may get destroyed if kept on heat for too long.

How should you use fresh herbs?

Herbs should preferably be torn with hands and not chopped with a knife as on doing so, they discolour and also do not release their full aroma. Mint and Basil make the dish more flavourful if the leaves are torn into smaller pieces with the hands.

How to store fresh coriander?

Wash coriander and put on a paper towel or tissue to absorb any excess water. Leave for 5 minutes. Place a paper towel or a paper napkin and place in a box. Put the washed coriander in the box lined with paper. Cover with the lid and keep in the fridge for a week or so.

Grow your own mint in pots!

Plant some thick shoots of mint in a pot, from the bunch you just purchased. Very soon it spreads and then just pluck leaves off as you need them.

What is bouquet garni?

This is a bundle or parcel of fresh herbs or spices tied in a muslin/cheese cloth. This bundle is put in soups, curries and sauces to flavour them during cooking. You can make up your own version of bouquet garni using any combination of spices and herbs like cardamoms, cinnamon, cloves and bay leaf. It is discarded from the cooked dish before serving.

One exception...

Herbs should be used fresh whenever possible, oregano being the one exception, as for some reason it has an even better flavour when dried.

CONVERSION GUIDE

These are not exact equivalents; they've been rounded-off to make measuring easier.

WEIGHTS AND MEASURES

FOOD STUFF	MEASURE	WEIGHT (GM)	FOOD STUFF	MEASURE	WEIGHT (GM)
Rice	1 cup	125	Cashewnut	6 large	10
Atta (wheat flour)	1 cup	100	Walnut	4 halves	10
Maida (plain flour)	1 cup	100	Raisins	1 tbsp	10
Suji	1 cup	120	Pista	1 tbsp (18 pcs)	10
Average for all dals	1/3 cup	50	Desiccated coconut	1/2 cup	25
Rajmah	1 cup	125	Cocoa powder	1 tbsp	5
Channa	1 cup	125	Coffee powder	1 tbsp	2
Besan	3/4 cup	50	Custard powder	1 tbsp	6
Milk	1 cup	200	Cornflour	1 tbsp	6
Milk Powder	1/4 cup	20	Creamed Corn	1 tbsp	17
Cheese grated	1 tbsp	5	Gelatine	1 tbsp	5
Butter	1 cup	150	Sugar	3/4 cup	100
	1 tbsp	15	Icing Sugar	1/4 cup	30
Curd	1/2 cup	100	Kheera (cucumber)	1 medium	150
	1 tbsp	15	Peas	10 Pods	50 (25 edible)
Cream	1/2 cup	100	French beans	13	50
	1 tbsp	15	Ginger	1" piece	10
Refined oil	1 cup	150	Tomato	1 medium	50
	1 tbsp	15	Potato	1 medium	70
Ghee	1 cup	180	Onion	1 medium	60
	1 tbsp	15	Cauliflower	1 medium	400
Ground nuts	1 tbsp (37 pcs)	10	Mushroom	7 medium	100
	1/4 cup	40	Cabbage	1 medium	400
Almonds	9 big	10	Carrot	1 medium	60

INTERNATIONAL CONVERSIONS

DRY MEASURES

METRIC	IMPERIAL
15 g	½ oz
30 g	1 oz
250 g	8 oz (½ lb)
500 g	16 oz (1 lb)
750 g	24 oz (1½ lb)
1 kg	32 oz (2 lb)

LIQUID MEASURES

METRIC	IMPERIAL
30 ml	1 fluid oz
60 ml	2 fluid oz
100 ml	3 fluid oz
150 ml	5 fluid oz (¼ pint/1 gill)
250 ml	8 fluid oz
300 ml	10 fluid oz (½ pint)
500 ml	16 fluid oz
1000 ml (1 litre)	1¾ pints

OVEN TEMPERATURES

These oven temperatures are only a guide; lower degree of heat are given. Always check the manufacturer's manual.

	°C (Celsius)	°F (Fahrenheit)	Gas Mark
Very slow	120	250	1
Slow	150	300	2
Moderately slow	160	325	3
Moderate	180	350	4
Moderately hot	190	375	5
Hot	200	400	6
Very hot	230	450	7

FAQS: FREQUENTLY ASKED QUESTIONS

What makes cabbage smell and stink?

In a nutshell the answer is over cooking. The sooner you get it out of the pan, the better. Cook it just until it is tender, 5-7 minutes, and it will keep its fresh sweet flavour.

How to remove excess moisture from vegetables after washing?

Pat dry on a kitchen towel and then roll in it to dry it well. If there is too much moisture in the vegetable, it tends to get mushy when cooked. Vegetables like spinach, cauliflower and ladys finger must specially be wiped well to get a crunchy dish.

What is the best way to squeeze lemon juice from lemons?

Always place a strainer over the cup to avoid the bitter seeds from going into the juice or the drink.

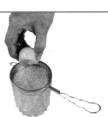

Working with raw onions!

If you find it difficult to cut the onion because of the "crying juices", cut into half and put in a bowl of water for 15 minutes before cutting. Peel the onion from the stem end first, since the root end releases more of those juices, that makes us cry.

No aluminium pans for spinach!

Aluminium creates a metallic reaction with spinach. Use stainless steel knives and pots or non stick pots.

How to wash greens like spinach or mustard (sarson)?

Submerge greens in a big pan full of water. Turn them around in water so that any particles of grit or sand clinging to them fall to the bottom. **Lift** up the leaves out of water and put in another pan of water. Discard the water which is dirty. Never **strain** the leaves or you will carry the dirt back in the leaves. Repeat the process with fresh water, until the water is no longer dirty.

Can you still use the garlic/onion if it has a green shoot coming out of the top?

By the time a green shoot is coming out of the top of the garlic/onion, that garlic/onion is almost flavourless. It can be used but the flavour is very little.

100% sure the cauliflower is free of any insects!

When I am not too sure about the cauliflower, specially during summers or the rainy season, I just boil half a pan of water with 2 tsp salt. Add cauliflower pieces to the boiling water. Remove from fire. I let the cauliflower sit in salted water for 10 minutes and then remove them from the water with a slotted spoon/flat spoon with holes (chhara). **Never strain! You might carry the insects back with the vegetable.** Put the cauliflower in tap water to stop heat from making it mushy. Pat dry on a clean kitchen towel and use.

Did you wash your hands after cutting green chillies?

If by accident you happen to touch your eyes, you'll just be crying and not cooking.

Sugar in some savoury dishes makes them tastier!

Sometimes a pinch of sugar makes a great difference to a vegetable. Vegetables like spinach (paalak paneer) or brinjals which carry a hint of bitterness taste better if a little sugar is added to them. Also, in tomato based curries, a pinch or two of sugar is more than welcome.

Is the long stalk of broccoli edible?

The broccoli head usually has a long, 4" stalk, and you should discard the bottom 2" of the stalk. To use the rest of the stalk, you may need to peel it if it looks too hard. Peeling is optional. Cut the rest of the stalk into round, thin slices and use it with the broccoli florets.

How to get that vivid green colour of broccoli? Is it by blanching?

Even if the broccoli is to be sauteed or baked, blanching it (putting it in hot water for 2 minutes) enhances and maintains the vegetables vivid colour. Boil a pan of water. Put the broccoli florets in it and remove the pan from fire. Let the vegetable be in hot water for 2 minutes. Strain. Pat dry on a kitchen towel and proceed as the recipe says.

Acid turns broccoli yellow!

Acidic ingredients like lemon juice or vinegar should be added to broccoli just before serving, as they turn the vivid green colour to yellow.

Crunchy Bhindi...

Add salt at the end of cooking as salt releases moisture which does not let the bhindi (okra) turn crisp and infact turns it into a mushy mess. Also wipe dry the vegetable well before cooking. Water present makes it slimy.

The mushroom dish wasn't enough for the party...

Mushrooms contain 85% water, so expect shrinkage and plan your purchase to allow for it. For e.g., 6 cups of thickly sliced mushrooms will be only 2 cups after cooking.

Waxy mashed potatoes!

When mashing boiled potatoes, don't over mash them and make them turn into a tasteless paste. The best way to mash them is to grate the boiled potato and mix gently with a fork to mash them.

To peel or not to peel eggplants/brinjals?

No, you should not peel. The skin is edible and it helps maintain the shape of brinjals.

How to remove the bitter taste in brinjals?

Brinjals have a bitter flavour, salting them before cooking helps drain out the bitterness. If the brinjals are cooked for very long, the bitterness usually evaporates, so there is no need to salt them before. However, if these are baked or fried which are short cooking processes, it is advisable to salt them. To do so, cut brinjals as desired, sprinkle some salt and toss. Keep aside for 10-15 minutes to sweat. Drain, rinse, pat dry and use as required.

How to quickly blanch tomatoes?

To skin tomatoes, cut a small shallow X on the bottom, put in a bowl and pour boiling water on them to cover. Keep for 3 minutes and then plunge into cold water. The skins will slip off easily. You can also put the 'X' marked tomatoes in a microproof bowl without water. 3 tomatoes need to be microwaved for 2½ minutes.

Those tender, freshly boiled, yellow sweet corn kernels...Did you know that corn gets tough on over cooking?

Boil a large pan of water with 1 tsp sugar, 1 tsp salt and a pinch of haldi for that beautiful yellow colour. Remove the husk and the silks of the corn cob and drop into the pan of boiling water. If the pan is small, you can break the corn cob into two pieces. Allow the water to return to a boil, boil for about 4-5 minutes only. Remove from fire. Let the corn remain in this water for 10 minutes. Remove with tongs (chimta) and let cool. Scrape the kernels with a knife.

How much kernels would 1 corn-on-the-cob give?

1 large corn on the cob will give ½ cup of boiled or roasted corn kernels.

How do I keep the left over ready made tomato puree?

These days readymade tomato puree is easily available and I like to use it as I find it very convenient. The puree is kept in the fridge. After using the required amount, it can be left in the tetra pack for 3-4 days. For longer storage, transfer the left over puree in a plastic/steel box and keep it in the freezer. It lasts well for a month or so.

I prefer the fresh tomato puree to the readymade one. How do I substitute in the recipes?

You may substitute ½ cup readymade puree with fresh puree of 3 tomatoes which is about 1 cup. Remember to cook it for a longer time as the ready made one is precooked.

Ginger paste is a little cumbersome, any substitute?

You can grate ginger instead. Remember to use the fine holes on the grater and grate into small shreds.

Fresh coconut can be stored in the freezer up to 3 months!

Enjoy fresh coconut chutney or a chicken korma without having to run around to buy a coconut everytime. Reserve the leftover coconut pieces in a zip lock bag in the freezer.

If you keep almonds or cashews in the cupboard for a couple of months, you might regret it...

Almonds, cashews, walnuts or even desiccated coconut, all have oil in them. Warm temperatures make the oil turn rancid, giving a peculiar, unedible taste to the nuts.

How do you pick a watermelon?

Look for a yellow oval patch on the top or bottom of it - that means it stayed longer on the vine (that side of the watermelon saw no sun and is riper).

Bad oil!

Cooking oil breaks down after several uses and acquires an off taste. To avoid this, always add some fresh oil to the used oil before frying. Also try and finish the once used oil in cooking vegetables /meat. Do not keep oil for frying separately.

How hot should the oil be before frying and how much oil to fill in the kadhai for frying?

Fill the kadhai a little less than half with oil. You should never fry in very hot or smoking hot oil. If the oil gets too hot, remove from fire and wait for 2 minutes. If the food is added to very hot oil it can turn into a dark mess. Also frying in oil which is not hot enough makes the food absorb a lot of oil!

You want to keep the yolks out of the whites or the whites won't beat up properly! ... Separating Eggs for cakes and desserts.

It is best to separate eggs when they are cold. The yolks have a tendency to break up if they are warm. Crack the shell with a blunt knife and pass the yolk back and forth between the broken shells while letting the white drip into a bowl beneath.

Another way to separate eggs, my preferred way, is to use your impeccably clean hands. The egg white falls cleanly and completely through your fingers. Try it, but make sure your hands are well washed first.

How to wash mince (keema)?

Place a strainer over a medium bowl. Spoon mince into strainer and add 1-2 cups water. Do not wash under running water. Press well to discard all water.

Why is home cooked chicken not as tender as in a restaurant?

Stir-fry chicken over medium heat with a turner or large spoon, lifting and stirring constantly for the first 3-4 minutes. Very high heat toughens the protien in the chicken making it hard. Then cover and cook on low heat till done. Use **fresh** chicken. **Frozen** is not that tender.

Crushing biscuits or almonds...

Place a few biscuits or almonds or any nuts in a plastic bag and crush with a rolling pin. You can use these wherever chopped nuts are required.

How to keep the rice grains separate?

1-2 tsp lemon juice may be added when the rice is cooking, to whiten and separate the rice grains. After the rice is cooked, gently fluff it with a fork to let the steam escape, so that the grains do not stick to each other.

How to boil chicken to get chicken shreds for sandwiches and salads?

Put chicken in a pan or pressure cooker with about ½ cup water and ½ tsp salt. After the boil comes or the pressure is formed, keep covered on low heat for 5-7 minutes till soft.

Something missing? ...Salt

Many a times the dish doesn't taste perfect. You feel something is missing. You may add a pinch of this or that spice and yet find something lacking. Try adding some salt and you will be surprised to taste the dish. It's perfect! Generally for 4 servings 1 tsp of salt is used when it is a dish with gravy and ¾ tsp is used for a dry or semi dry dish. If in doubt about the amount it is always better to use less salt and then add more later if you feel the need. This is just a guide.

PULSES (LENTILS & LEGUMES)

(Dals, Rajmah, Channa & other Dried Beans)

Pulses store well for 2-3 months. If you keep them longer, they harbour insects. Keep them in tightly sealed jars or bottles in a dry place.

Dals can be whole or skinned. Whole dals (saboot dals) have a dark covering on them and need more cooking time. Skinned dals (dhuli dals) are without the hard cover and split into two and thus cook much faster. Moong dal is green when whole or saboot and yellow when skinned and is called dhuli moong. Similarly urad saboot is black whereas dhuli urad is whitish. Masoor saboot is reddish brown and dhuli masoor is orangish in colour. Although dhuli masoor dal is orangish in colour, on cooking it becomes yellow.

POPULAR PULSES

Masoor Saboot (Whole Red Lentils)

Masoor Dhuli (Skinned, Split Red Lentils)

Urad Saboot (Whole Black Lentils)

Urad Dhuli (Skinned, Split Black Lentils)

Moong Saboot (Whole Moong Beans)

Moong Dhuli (Skinned, Split Moong Beans)

Channe ki Dal (Gram Lentils)

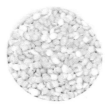

Arhar/Toor (Yellow Lentils)

Kale Channe (Black Chickpeas)

Safed or Kabuli Channe (White Chickpeas)

Rajmah (Kidney Beans)

Lobia (Black-eyed Bean)

I forgot to soak the rajmah at night? My husband/ boyfriend/ brother wants to eat rajmah-chawal this afternoon...

Use the famous quick soak method. Mix rajmah with tap water to cover and bring to a boil. Keep on low heat for 2 minutes, remove from fire and keep aside covered for 1 hour.

Do I use the same water to boil the channas in which they were soaked?

Soaking water should be discarded and the channas boiled with fresh water to avoid indigestion. Soaking helps to breakdown and leach out the indigestible complex sugars called oligosaccharide in whole dals, rajmah (beans) and channas (chick peas), that may cause intestinal ramblings.

I want my channas to be of a dark brown colour on cooking...

Add 1-2 tea bags or 2 tsp of tea leaves tied in a piece of cloth to the channas when you put it to boil. The tea gives colour. Discard the tea bag after the channas are cooked.

Should you add baking soda (mitha soda) when boiling rajmah?

Baking soda shortens the cooking time but it robs the rajmah of its vitamin B content. So better to avoid it.

How much water to add to get a good dal?

If 1 cup dal is to be cooked, add 3-4 cups water to it, depending on the type of dal. For skinned dals (**dhuli dals**), 3 cups water is enough where as for the whole dals (**saboot dals**), another extra cup is needed. For beans (**rajmah**) and chickpeas (**channas**) add 5 cups of water for every 1 cup of rajmah or channas.

Do black eyed beans (lobia) need to be soaked overnight?

They cook well without soaking for too long. 30 minutes of soaking is enough. Soak first thing and while the masala is being prepared, they will be ready to cook.

How to get a reddish dal makhani? Mine is always blackish.

Soak whole black beans (kali dal) overnight or for 5-6 hours. Drain the water. Add fresh water. Scrub the dal well. Discard water and you will see that it is blackish. Wash and rub dal well in fresh changes of water till you see that the water is no longer blackish. Use dry red chillies instead of chilli powder for a fiery red colour.

Extra Salt...

Not to worry! Add a few drops of lemon juice or a few pinches of sugar and see the difference in the taste. Also you can add a peeled, whole potato to it which absorbs the extra salt.

RICE & WHEAT

Mainly the long grained basmati rice is used for pullaos and biryani. But for every day use, you could buy the smaller basmati rice, which is fragrant, but not very long grained. Rice stores well for 2-3 months in tightly sealed jars. Make sure that no moisture or insects get into the rice.

Whole wheat flour (atta), plain flour (maida) and semolina (suji) are all processed from wheat. Whole wheat flour can be stocked for a month or more. When you refill your canister of whole wheat flour, always wash and then wipe well. Dry properly before refilling it. Never use a wet utensil to take out the amount needed. Put a small bowl in the canister to take out for every day use.

There are so many brands of wheat flour in the market, which one is better?

It is best to buy the quality which has more fibre. Very white wheat flour is not healthy as it looks. It is more like maida (plain flour) and lacks fibre, although the chappatis made from such flour may look attractive.

What is the best way to store maida (plain flour) and suji (semolina) ?

Store in jars in the fridge as they harbour insects very easily if kept in a warm place. Do not buy large quantities at a time.

Can you make phulkas immediately with the dough which is just kneaded?

No, knead dough well till smooth and keep it covered for half an hour before using. If this is not done, its puffing quality is affected and the edges become cracked. Do not use too much dry flour in rolling the dough, the roti might turn dry. Use a heavy griddle for cooking chapatis and paranthas.

Should you soak rice before cooking?

The traditional way is to soak rice for 20-30 minutes before cooking. But I have experienced that soaking makes the rice extra soft and so there are great chances for the grains to break when the rice is sauteed in oil when making a pullao. The best way is to wash the rice in a soup strainer and let it be in the strainer for 20-30 minutes. The rice stays moist in the strainer and remains full grained on cooking.

What sort of pan is ideal for cooking rice?

A big, deep pan (patila) with a heavy bottom is ideal. Also see that it has a well fitting lid. Nonstick deep pans with well fitting lids are ideal.

Why place a tawa underneath a pan of rice while cooking ?

Rice cooks best when the heat is very low. Putting a tawa beneath the pan of rice will reduce the heat to a minimum and will ensure that the rice grains are fully cooked when all the water has been absorbed. But always bring the rice to a boil first and then place the tawa beneath the pan of simmering rice.

Fork or Spoon?

When you transfer the rice to the serving platter, use a fork to do so. The spoon might mash the rice grains, whereas the fork on the contrary will fluff up the rice, separating the rice grains.

Chicken:

BUYING & STORING:

* Do not buy a chicken with yellow skin & flesh. Buy one with white skin & flesh.
* Prefer picking fresh chicken to frozen.
* Never re-freeze thawed out chicken, as it will turn hard and tough on cooking.

COOKING:

* Do not over cook chicken. It tends to get hard.
* Use moderate to low heat for tender, juicy and uniformly cooked chicken.
* Marinate chicken for grilling and tandoori recipes. It helps to tenderize the meat.
* For steaks and dishes where the full breast is cooked, cover the breast with cling wrap and pound (hit) it with a rolling pin or a meat mallet. The breast gets thin and cooks faster.
* Do not keep left over at room temperature. Refrigerate it as soon as possible.
* If the chicken is frozen, thaw and marinate only in the refrigerator, never at room temperature. So if the chicken is in the freezer, and you want to cook it the next morning, remove from freezer and put it in the upper shelf of the refrigerator (coldest part of the fridge) at night.

Working with raw poultry...

After working with raw poultry you should wash your cutting board, knives and hands well with hot soapy water before touching any other food. And remember wooden cutting boards are porous and can harbour bacteria more conveniently, so go in for plastic ones or other non porous ones for cutting poultry.

Getting familiar with different cuts of chicken

Wings

Chicken pieces with bone

Chicken drumsticks (legs)

Breast fillets

Mutton

BUYING: Pale pink flesh indicates young lamb or goat and the flesh darkens as its age increases. As a general rule, the younger the lamb the more tender it is. The creamy white fat turns yellow as the animal grows older.
COOKING: Use constant moderate to low temperature for cooking meat. High temperatures toughen the protein, squeeze out the juices and cause excessive shrinkage. Marinate less tender cuts of meat in raw papaya, kachari, vinegar, curd, sour milk or cook in tomato juice to hasten change of collagen to gelatine which makes the meat tender. Meat for grilling or tandoori should be at room temperature before beginning.

Getting familiar with different varieties of mutton

Mutton chops

Boneless mutton

Mutton mince

Fish & Seafood:

BUYING:

- If possible, buy fish that are displayed on crushed ice and preferably not prewrapped.
  The flesh of the whole fish should be firm to touch. If your finger leaves a depression, the fish is not fresh enough to eat. The eyes should be clear, bright and shiny and not dull or sunken. It should not have a strong fishy odour.

STORING:

- Fish is very perishable, so do not roam around after buying fish. Buy it at the end of your shopping. If the commuting time is too much, put ice in the bag which has fish. Once you get home, refrigerate immediately in the freezer. Cook it the same day or at most, a day later. Store uncooked in the refrigerator for not more than 1-2 days.

COOKING:

- To remove the fishy odour, rub a little lemon juice, salt and turmeric (haldi) on the fish and keep aside for at least 15-20 minutes. Wash and proceed.
- Cook fish only till tender, till it falls easily into clumps of snowy white flakes when tested with a fork. Fish cooks very quickly because it has very little connective tissue. Cook prawns only for 2-3 minutes, stirring frequently. Prawns and shrimp turn pink and become firm when done. Never over cook.
- Always cook fish at low temperatures. High temperature tends to toughen fish.
- When thawing frozen fish, run the packet under cold water until thawed. Do not thaw at room temperature or under warm water. Never re-freeze fish once it has been thawed

CUTS OF FISH

Fish Steaks

Fish steaks are the cross section of a large pan-dressed fish. Steaks are ½ to ¾" thick. Allow 100-150 gm per serving.

Fish Fillets

Fish Fillets are the sides of the fish, cut lengthwise from the fish. They can be purchased with or without skin. Fillets usually are boneless; however, small bones, called pins, may be present. Allow 100-150 gm per serving.

How do you get rid of that fishy odour from your hands after cooking fish?

After you have finished handling the fish, your hands acquire a fishy odour which is hard to lose. The perfect solution is to rub your hands with toothpaste and rinse them off. It works!

Eggs:

BUYING & STORING:

- Buy fresh eggs (a little transparent fuzzy shell), heavy, free from cracks.

COOKING:

- Avoid high temperatures and too rapid-cooking. Do not overcook.
- Beat egg whites with a clean beater in a clean bowl. Not even a trace of fat or egg yolk should be present, it you want the eggwhites to turn really fluffy.
- Beat egg whites immediately before use. Fold in carefully into mixtures.

Confused... scared about the party coming up! Follow the easy-to-do menu and the party is a sure shot hit.

The Welcome Drink - Fill the glass with ice first and then pour the drink over it. A day before the party, make some ice cubes of the juice itself with mint or apple dices (tiny pieces) frozen in it. Natural juices may be served plain or whipped up with some ginger juice or ginger ale or lime cordial, a few tbsp of cream and crushed ice. Keep some extra drink in a jug (pitcher) in summers on the table. Don't forget the ice bucket!

Snack/Starter - Offering two appetizers makes the guests feel special. Keep them bite sized (small). See that both are not fried. Mexican bean bites and Amritsar paneer make a great pair. If you don't have enough time to prepare the second snack, simply cut sticks of cucumber, radish, carrots or even apples and serve with a cheese dip dressed up with freshly crushed peppercorns. Relax at the time of serving snacks, don't rush. Serve one at a time and with some time gap in between. But don't wait too long before serving dinner or your guests may fill up on nibbles and have no room left.

The Main Dish - See that it is universally liked. The quantity should be more than the other dishes. It should be a thick gravy. Hyderabadi korma or shahi malai kofta or even butter chicken will be good. Garnish it imaginatively. It makes all the difference!

Side Dishes - Buffet parties being in vogue, dry or semi dry side dishes are more practical. The dishes don't run into each other. The quantity should be less. Don't keep too many dishes, two are enough with the main dish.

Special Dish - One special dish may be a Continental bake or a cold salad with a good dressing in summers, or even delicious dahi badas with chutney.

Roti and Rice - You may buy tandoori rotis or rumali rotis from outside if you do not have enough help. It saves a lot of botheration and unnecessary tension.
Paranthas can be made in advance and fried at serving time. Use a tissue while frying to absorb excess oil. No one really likes the oily look!

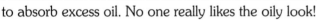

Dessert - When guests are finished or have almost finished eating, start getting ready for serving dessert, but don't clear the table until everyone is done eating. End with a quick dessert but garnish it differently. Serve some chocolates with coffee at the end

HOW CAN I MAKE MY PARTY FUN?

For most parties, just getting together is all you'll need to do. But if your guests don't know each other well, here are some ways to break the ice:

Introduce guests to each other as soon as they arrive. Get the conversation rolling by bringing up some topics you know your friends have in common.

Let your guests help by pouring drinks or lighting candles. Some people are more comfortable if they're helping instead of being waited on.

Don't forget the music! It could be jazz, classical gazals, filmi... Just keep the sound level at low moderate so everyone can enjoy the conversation.

Plan a fun activity for everyone to do together—it could be games like parcing the parcel; singing; or a sport if your party is outdoors.

PLATES AND CUP

Soup/fruit bowl

Salad/Quarter plate

Dinner/Full plate

Cup and Saucer

Charger Plate

FLATWARE (CUTLERY)

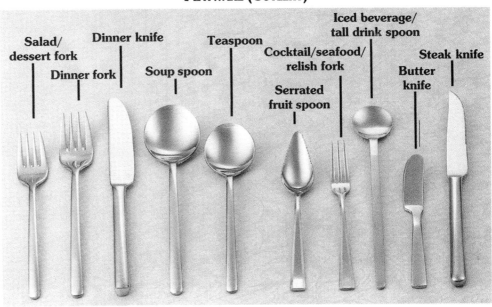

Salad/dessert fork

Dinner fork

Dinner knife

Soup spoon

Teaspoon

Serrated fruit spoon

Cocktail/seafood/relish fork

Iced beverage/tall drink spoon

Butter knife

Steak knife

GLASSES AND SPECIALTY GLASSES FOR COCKTAILS AND MIXED DRINKS

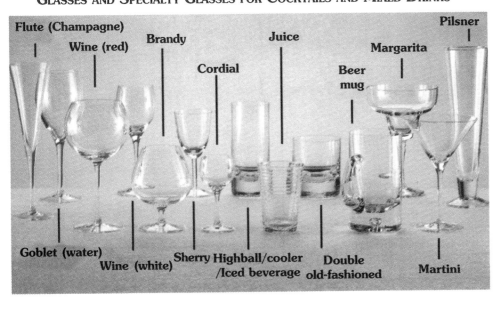

Flute (Champagne)

Wine (red)

Brandy

Cordial

Juice

Beer mug

Margarita

Pilsner

Goblet (water)

Wine (white)

Sherry

Highball/cooler/Iced beverage

Double old-fashioned

Martini

43

TABLE- SETTING

You've picked your menu and figured out how much food to buy, but how do you actually serve the meal? Basically, there are two main serving styles: **sit-down & buffet. The table is set according to the way in which you want to serve your guests or family.**

SIT-DOWN MEAL

Casual setting for a family meal

Formal setting for a meal

Here's a quick refresher course for setting the table for a sit-down meal:

Full Plates (Dinner Plate) should be placed about 1" from the edge of the table with the forks on the left and the knife (blade toward the plate) and spoon to the right.

Bread & Butter Plates if used, should be placed almost above the forks with the butter knife on it.

Quarter (Salad Plates) are placed to the left of the forks in line with the full (dinner) plate.

Flatware (Cutlery) pieces used first are placed farthest from the plate. For example, if salad is served first, the salad fork goes to the left of the dinner fork. As you use your utensils for each course, you work your way in towards the plate.

Glassware is arranged above the knife. The water glass is usually at the tip of the knife, with beverage and/or wine glasses to the right of the water glass.

Napkins can be placed either on the center of the dinner plate or quarter plate or tucked inside the water glass. Interesting ways to fold napkins follow later.

Dessert Plates and Spoons are usually brought to the table with dessert.

Cups and Saucers for coffee and tea, if serving with the main meal, are placed slightly above and to the right of the spoons. Or they can be brought out later when dessert is served.

Heating and Chilling plates

One of the rules that was repeated over and over when I was at the Lady Irwin College of Delhi was "Serve hot food on hot plates and cold food on cold plates." It really makes a difference in keeping your food the temperature you want it to be. It also makes an impression on your guests. Put the heap of plates in the microwave (ensure they are microproof!) to warm them before you arrange them on the table. If possible, put your dessert plates in the fridge at least 30 minutes before you are ready to serve a cold dessert.

BAD MANNERS!
Never seat a guest facing the wall.

BUFFET

We generally prefer buffet when the number of guests is large. All the food and crockery are arranged in a central place and guests help themselves. **At dinner time, it is good manners to hand out the plates to the guests!**

Consider your menu. Since you cannot have too many katoris or small bowls for gravy dishes, do not keep too many items which are runny.

If you're inviting a very large group, plan to have two platters for each food. When one platter is almost empty, you can fix up the next one and make a quick switch. If the food you are serving is cold or room temperature, you can even prepare the second platter ahead of time.

Remember to have enough place for everyone to sit. Buffets are great if you don't have one table that's big enough to seat all of your guests. But you still need enough spots for people to sit down.

Table placement is the secret to a guest-friendly buffet. Put the buffet in the center of the room, so guests can help themselves from all sides of the table. For a large group, set up identical lines on each side of the table. Or push the table against the wall to save space, leaving three sides open for serving.

If your table is small you can use a separate table or counter to lay out the glasses or beverages where guests can serve themselves. This also avoids a traffic jam around food.

How to arrange the food?

The dishes that go together (rice and curry) are near each other. This way, guests can help themselves without backtracking.

Place the crockery and flatware at the start of the table. Keep both spoons and forks neatly arranged. Stack the plate with the napkin placed between each plate.

Pretend you're a guest and walk through your set up buffet table. You'll quickly find out what adjustments you need to make!

A Disaster - I can't Forget!

When I gave my first party, I cooked some dishes in the morning and kept putting them aside in the kitchen. At serving time, I was shocked to see that the gravies, specially the dishes which had tomatoes in them were almost at the point of getting spoilt. A few more hours of lying outside and they would have gone into the dust bin. So on a hot summer day, keep putting all the cooked dishes in the fridge. Take them out an hour before serving.

NAPKIN FOLDS

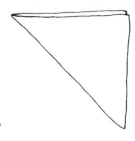

GOBLET TWIST

1. Fold napkin in half diagonally into a triangle. Roll up tightly from the edge of the dotted line.

2. Fold in half and place in goblet.

SILVERWARE HOLDER

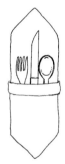

1. Fold the napkin into quarters. Position napkin so that the open four points are at the top. Roll down top corner a little as shown.

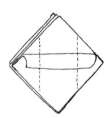

2. Roll down the folded corner further, almost about half way as shown. Now fold the opposite sides on the dotted line.

3. Tuck silverware into the napkin's "pocket."

THE FAN

1. Open the napkin to full size. Fold in half, bringing the left edge to the right edge. Starting at the bottom, make accordion pleats two-thirds of the way up.

3. Fold the overlap on the left towards the front.

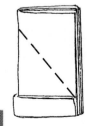

2. Fold in half with the accordion pleating on the outside. Fold on the dotted line, laying the right side along the accordion pleat.

4. Rest the overlap on the table or plate, and let the fan open so its facing towards you.

COOKING PREPARATIONS

These may sound boring but once you inculcate these habits, they'll prove very useful in the long run. And a bonus - your mother in law is sure to get impressed by these qualities!

How to organise work without wasting time, fuel and nutrition ?

1. Keep the area clean and uncluttered all the time. Put away any utensil or ingredients not required. Clean and wash up side by side if possible.
2. Keep foods under cover all the time to protect them from dust and insects.
3. The door of the refrigerator is the warmest part of the fridge. Things which are easily perishable should not be kept in the door. Jams and chutneys are best for the door.
3. Begin with the dish that requires longest time for preparation.
4. Wash fruits and vegetables before use. Peel vegetables and fruits as thinly as possible. Throw waste material into the dust bin.
6. Use a pair of tongs (sansi) for handling hot utensils and oven gloves for taking out dishes from the oven.
7. Do not put the spoon back into the food after tasting the food.
9. Serve food in the dish neatly. Remove traces or spots of food from the rim of the serving dish with a paper napkin or a damp cloth.

ESSENTIAL COOKING TIPS

For baking, should the oven be preheated and for how long?

It is necessary to preheat the oven to the temperature at which you are going to bake. Set the temperature of the oven at which you want to bake and generally when the oven reaches that temperature, it beeps! If it does not beep, then just preheat the oven for 10-12 minutes.

Where should the food be placed in the oven - top rack or in the middle?

The distance from the heat to the food is important. If the food is too close to the heat, it will burn. Preferably the middle rack or even the last one is good.

How do you steam without a steamer basket?

To steam, fill a deep pan with a little water, say upto 1" level. Keep it on fire to boil the water. Put a steel strainer (colander) on the pan of water. Put the food as it is or in another utensil like a thali for dhokla, on the strainer and cover the strainer with a lid. Lower the heat to medium. Do not steam on very low heat as the water will not boil and no steam will form.

How much oil should I put in the kadhai for frying?

Fill the kadhai a little less than half with oil. If there is too much oil, it bubbles and flows over. If it is too little, the food is not fried properly.

What is the right way to fry?

Heat oil in a kadhai, but if it starts to smoke, shut off heat. Let it cool down a bit and return to heat. Dry your food well before frying. Fry in batches as too much food in the oil lowers the temperature of the oil and the food absorbs a lot of oil if the oil is not hot enough.

What is the right way to saute any vegetable/meat ?

Food is tossed and stir fried in a shallow pan in a small amount of oil/fat. Whether you are sauteing in a kadhai or a non stick pan, the most important point to remember is to keep the food spaced out. Do not overlap the vegetable/meat while sauteing. Keep them spread out in a single layer and you'll be amazed to see how crisp and crunchy the food remains with this little trick!

What is the difference between grilling and baking?

During baking, there is uniform heat all around where as in grilling there is direct heat only from the top or bottom. So for cakes, baking is done whereas to melt cheese or for browning the top of baked dishes, the grilling mode is preferred.

How do you flatten chicken breasts?

Flatten chicken breast to ¼" thickness between sheets of plastic wrap, lightly pounding with the flat side of a meat mallet or a rolling pin/belan.

I want the crispy coating on my snack! what to do ?

Dredge the snack with dry maida first by rolling it over maida spread out in a plate. Now dip it in egg wash which is 2 tbsp egg white mixed with 2 tbsp water. If you do no take eggs, dip in plain water. Finally coat the snack with bread crumbs which will now stick better. Any time you coat something with bread crumbs, the crumbs will stick even better if you give the coated item a little chilling-out time in the fridge, for atleast 15 minutes. A tsp of sesame seeds (til), or a little of carom seeds (ajwain) or some mustard powder added to the crumbs make the food more appetizing.

How to whip cream without it getting curdled?

An electric hand mixer is best for whipping cream. The cream and the beater should be properly chilled. Also transfer the cream to the right size of the pan/bowl in which it can be whipped comfortably, so that the utensil is also cold along with the cream. During hot weather, beat cream over ice. A few drops of lemon juice added to the cream will whip cream faster and prevent curdling.

Roasting of nuts enhances their flavour!

Toasting nuts enhances flavour. Toast them on fire in an ungreased pan or microwave them for 2-3 minutes. You may spread nuts in an ungreased baking tray and bake uncovered at 180°C/350°F in the oven for about 10 minutes, stirring occasionally, until golden brown and fragrant. Watch carefully because nuts brown quickly.

Need dry bread crumbs urgently?

Break 2 bread slices into small pieces. Spread out on a plate and microwave for 2 minutes. Mix the bread in the plate with the hands to change sides. Microwave for another 1 minute. Remove from microwave and keep aside for 5 minutes to dry. Grind in a mixer to get instant crumbs.

What are fresh crumbs?

To make fresh bread crumbs, tear bread into small pieces. Churn in a mixer grinder to get fresh crumbs.

TERMS USED IN COOKING

Al Dente: Doneness description for pasta cooked until tender but firm to the bite.

Bake: Cook in oven surrounded by dry heat. Bake uncovered for dry, crisp surfaces (breads, cakes, cookies, chicken) or covered for moistness (casseroles, chicken, vegetables).

Baste: Spoon fat over food during cooking to keep it moist.

Batter: An uncooked mixture of flour, eggs and liquid in combination with other ingredients; thin enough to be poured as for pancakes.

Beat: Combine ingredients vigorously in a rotatory motion, with a wire whisk, hand beater or electric mixer or fork, until mixture is smooth and uniform.

Beat

Blanch

Blanch: Plunge food into boiling water for a brief time to preserve color, texture and nutritional value like blanching broccoli or to remove skin like blanching almonds or tomatoes.

Blend: Combine ingredients with spoon, wire whisk or rubber scraper until mixture is very smooth and uniform. A blender or food processor may also be used.

Boil: Heat liquid until bubbles rise continuously and break on the surface and steam is given off. For rolling boil, the bubbles form rapidly.

Brown: Cook quickly over high heat, causing food surface to turn brown.

Caramelize

Caramelize: Melt sugar slowly over low heat in a heavy bottom kadhai or a nonstick pan, until it becomes a golden brown, caramel-flavored syrup. Or sprinkle granulated, powdered or brown sugar on top of a food, then place under a broiler or grill until the sugar is melted and caramelized. Also a technique for cooking vegetables, especially onions, until golden brown.

Chill: Place food in the refrigerator until it becomes thoroughly cold, but not frozen.

Chop: Cut into coarse or fine irregular pieces, using knife, food chopper, blender or food processor.

Coat: Cover food evenly with maida, crumbs or sauce.

Consistency: The thickness or texture of a mixture.

Cool: Allow hot food to stand at room temperature for a specified amount of time. Placing hot food on a wire rack will help it cool more quickly. Stirring mixture occasionally also will help it cool more quickly and evenly.

Crush

Core: Remove the center of a fruit (apple, pear or pineapple). Cores contain small seeds (apple, pear) or have a woody texture (pineapple).

Cover: Place lid, plastic wrap or aluminum foil over a container of food.

Crisp-Tender: Doneness description of vegetables cooked until they retain some of the crisp texture of the raw food.

Crush: Press into very fine particles either in a mortar pestle or in a small spice grinder or on a chakla belan.

Cube: Cut food into squares ½ inch or larger, using knife.

Cut up: Cut into small irregular pieces with kitchen scissors or knife, or cut into smaller pieces.

Dash: Less than 1/8 tsp of an ingredient.

Deep-fry: Cook in hot fat that's deep enough to float the food.

Dice: Cut food into squares smaller than ½ inch, using knife.

Dip: Moisten or coat by plunging below the surface of a liquid, covering all sides (dipping onion ring into batter, dipping bread into egg mixture for french toast).

Dot: Drop small pieces of an ingredient (margarine, butter) randomly over food like in apple pie.

Dough: Mixture of flour and liquid in combination with other ingredients that is stiff but pliable. Dough can be dropped from a spoon (for cookies), rolled (for pie crust) or kneaded (for bread).

Drain: Pour off liquid by putting a food into a strainer or colander that has been set in the sink or over another container. When liquid is to be saved, place the strainer in a bowl or other container.

Drizzle: Pour sauce or topping in thin lines from a spoon or a squeeze bottle in an uneven pattern over food (glaze over cake or cookies, cream over curries or soups, chocolate sauce on ice cream).

Dust: Sprinkle lightly with flour, granulated sugar, powdered sugar or cocoa powder (dusting coffee cake with powdered sugar).

Flake: Break lightly into small pieces, using fork (cooked fish).

Flute: Squeeze pastry edge with fingers to make a finished, ornamental edge as in apple pie or tarts.

Flute

Fold

Fold: Combine mixtures lightly while preventing loss of air with a spoon. Gently spoon or pour one mixture over another mixture in a bowl. Using a rubber spatula, first cut down vertically through mixtures. Next, slide spatula across bottom of bowl and up outside the mixture, turning the bottom mixture over the top mixture. Rotate bowl one-fourth turn, and repeat this down across-up motion. Continue mixing in this way just until mixtures are blended (folding beaten egg yolks into beaten egg whites for souffle, folding liqueur into whipped cream).

Garnish: Decorate food with small amounts of other foods that have distinctive color or texture (parsley, fresh berries, carrot curls) to enhance appearance.

Glaze: Brush, spread or drizzle an ingredient or mixture of ingredients (meat stock, heated jam, melted chocolate) on hot or cold foods to give a glossy appearance or hard finish.

Grate: Rub a hard-textured food (chocolate, citrus peel, cheese, carrots, potatoes) against the small, rough sharp-edged holes of a grater. For citrus peel, grate only the skin, not the bitter white membrane.

Grease: Rub the bottom and sides of a pan with shortening (oil or butter), to prevent food from sticking during baking (muffins, some casseroles). Also may use cooking spray.

Preheat Oven: Turn the oven control(s) to the desired temperature, allowing the oven to heat thoroughly before adding food. Preheating takes about ten minutes for most ovens.

Julienne: Cut into thin, match-like strips, using knife or food processor (fruits, vegetables, meats).

Knead: Work dough on a floured surface, using hands or an electric mixer with dough hooks, into a smooth, elastic mass. Kneading develops the gluten in flour and results in breads, biscuits and other baked goods with an even texture and a smooth, rounded top. Kneading by hand can take up to about 15 minutes.

Knead

Marinate: Let food stand usually in refrigerator in a savoury mixture, usually acidic, in a glass or plastic container to add flavour or to tenderize the food. Marinade is the savoury liquid in which the food is marinated.

Melt: Turn a solid (chocolate, margarine) into liquid by heating.

Mince: Cut food into very fine pieces; smaller than chopped food.

Pan fry

Pan fry: Fry meat or other food starting with a cold skillet, using little or no fat and usually pouring off fat from meat as it accumulates during cooking.

Peel: Cut off outer covering, using knife or vegetable peeler (apples, potatoes). Also strip off outer covering, using fingers (bananas, oranges).

Puree: Mash or blend food until smooth and uniform consistency, using a blender or food processor or by forcing food through a sieve.

Rind: The outer skin of citrus fruits like lemon or orange. Lemon rind can be taken out by grating a firm lemon on the grater gently, so that only the outer yellow skin gets grated, leaving behind the white pith, which is bitter.

Rind

Saute: Cook in hot fat over medium-high heat with frequent tossing or turning motion.

Season: Add flavour, usually with salt, pepper, herb or spices.

Shred: Cut into long, thin pieces, using round, smooth holes of grater, a knife or a food processor (cabbage, carrots, cheese).

Sift: To pass dry ingredients through a fine sieve, either to incorporate air as in cake flour or to remove any foreign material or to remove any lumps as in icing sugar.

Sift

Simmer: Cook in liquid on gas top at just below the boiling point. Usually done after reducing heat from a boil. Bubbles will rise slowly and break just below the surface.

Skim: Remove fat or foam from a soup, curry, stock or stew, using a spoon or ladle.

Slice: Cut into uniform-size flat pieces (bread, meat).

Soft Dropping Consistency: The mixture is thick enough to be heaped in a spoon and soft enough to fall by itself when the spoon or beater is lifted. A thick mixture which drops from a spoon when it is lifted, without applying any force.

Soft peaks

Soft Peaks: Egg whites beaten until peaks are rounded or curl when beaters are lifted from bowl, while still moist and glossy. See also stiff peaks.

Soften: Let cold food stand at room temperature, or microwave at low power setting, until no longer hard (margarine, butter, cream cheese).

Steam

Steam: Cook food by placing in a colander (flat strainer with big holes) or a special steamer basket. Place the colander over boiling or simmering water in a pan. Cover the colander while steaming. Steaming helps retain flavour, shape, colour, texture and nutritional value.

Stew: Cook slowly in a small amount of liquid till soft (stewed fruit, beef stew).

Stiff Peaks: Egg whites beaten until peaks stand up straight when beaters are lifted from bowl, while still moist and glossy. See also Soft Peaks.

Stir: Combine ingredients with circular or figure-eight motion until uniform consistency. Stir once in a while for "stirring occasionally," stir often for "stirring frequently" and stir continuously for "stirring constantly."

Stir-fry: A Chinese method of cooking uniform pieces of food in small amount of hot oil over high heat, lifting and stirring constantly with a turner or large spoon.

Stone: To remove seeds, as in dates or cherries.

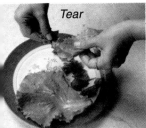
Tear

Strain: Pour mixture or liquid through a fine sieve or strainer.

Tear: Break into pieces, using fingers (lettuce for salad, bread slices for fresh bread crumbs).

Toast: Brown lightly, using toaster, oven, broiler or a tawa (griddle), like almonds, sesame seeds etc.

Toss: Tumble ingredients lightly with a lifting motion (salads).

Whip: Beat ingredients to add air and increase volume until ingredients are light and fluffy (whipping cream, egg whites).

Zest: Outside coloured peel of citrus fruit (oranges, lemons) that contains aromatic oils and flavor. Also, to remove outside colored layer of citrus fruit in fine strips, using knife, citrus zester or vegetable peeler. See rind.

BASIC RECIPES

How to Prepare Paneer

To make soft home made paneer, it is important to use good quality milk. Paneer prepared from full cream milk is certainly softer and tastier than that made from skimmed/toned milk.

To make paneer at home, take out juice of one lemon in a strainer put over a small bowl, to remove the seeds. The seeds taste bitter if they come in the paneer by mistake. If there is no lemon, keep one cup of curd ready.

 Boil one litre of full cream milk, stirring continuously to prevent skin forming at the top. When it comes to a boil, put off the fire. Add lemon juice or curd (yogurt). Return to low heat, stir gently, till all the milk curdles and the greenish water called whey separates. Remove from fire. Leave it covered for 15 minutes. Strain through a muslin cloth and squeeze out the whey. Do not squeeze too hard or you might get a very dry paneer.

If cubes of paneer are required, keep the paneer which is wrapped in the muslin cloth in a rectangular plastic/tiffin box. The paneer takes its shape. To get a compact brick of paneer, place a heavy weight on the paneer when it is in the box, for an hour or so. Remove the cloth and use the perfect home made paneer.

> **Soft Paneer**
>
> *Do not keep the milk on fire, after it curdles. Once the green water/whey separates, shut off the fire. If you keep boiling the milk after paneer is formed, the paneer gets tough.*

How to Set Yogurt (Dahi)

Boil ½ litre (2½ cups) milk. Let it cool down a bit till it is luke warm. Wash your hands well and put a finger in it to check. It should feel comfortably hot. Put ½ tsp of yogurt (starter/*khatta*) in a small clean deep bowl, the size which is enough to hold that quantity of milk. Do not take a very big bowl. Keeping the bowl with the starter yogurt on the table, pour the milk in a stream on it. Mix well. Pour the milk back into the pan and finally pour it back into the bowl. Mixing 2-3 times this way helps the starter to mix evenly with the milk. Keep in a place where it can sit undisturbed for 3-4 hours. If you disturb it in-between, it might not set or take much longer to set. As soon as the yogurt sets, keep in the fridge.

- In winters, heat the milk a little more and add extra starter.
- During winters, set the curd in narrow and high utensil instead of a broad one. Keep it in a warm place to set, may be inside the oven (without switching it on).

> *To give the raita a much stronger flavour, make it in advance and chill in the fridge until ready to serve.*

> **Yogurt/Dahi is still Milky**
>
> *If your dahi is still a little loose and not set properly even after 4-5 hours, microwave it for 1-2 minutes. Leave it undisturbed for 15-20 minutes and enjoy a firm yogurt. But it is important to use a microproof utensil for setting curd. Curd set in beautiful coloured pottery handis look good and they are microproof too!*

ONION PASTE

Onions are ground to a paste in a mixer-grinder for many dishes. If you are a working person, on the weekend you can make the paste and store it in the refrigerator. Use as required.

To make paste, chop onions roughly, grind them to a paste in a mixer without any water, stir fry paste in some oil till light golden. Let it cool and you can then store it in a box or a wide mouthed bottle for the whole week. 3 onions usually give 1 cup of raw onion paste. You need about 3-4 tbsp oil to stir fry the paste. Use a heavy bottomed kadhai or pan to stir fry onion paste because it sticks to the bottom. It needs to be stirred continuously or it gets brown unevenly.

When the onion paste is fried till golden and is ready to add the masalas, sprinkle 2 tbsp water on the onions to prevent it from turning dark brown. Also remember to reduce the heat, as high heat will ruin the flavour of the spices.

3 onions = 1 cup onion paste (raw)

TOMATO PUREE

Tomatoes are roughly chopped and ground to a puree in a mixer-grinder. Instead of using raw tomatoes they are sometimes blanched. Blanching means to put the tomatoes in boiling hot water for 3-4 minutes and then plunging them in cold or tap water. This loosens the skin which is then removed. The peeled and slightly cooked tomatoes are then churned in the mixer to give a bright red puree. In contrast if the tomatoes are not blanched, the raw tomatoes give a pinkish puree and also the colour of the curry is then not so bright. These days ready made tomato puree is easily available. 1 cup fresh puree can be substituted by ½ cup readymade puree.

Choose bright red tomatoes to get a good red curry. Sometimes the tomatoes are a little under ripe, they are yellowish from the stalk end. Such tomatoes yield a yellowish puree and you may be disappointed to see the final dish.

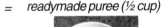

fresh puree (1 cup)   =   readymade puree (½ cup)

=

3 tomatoes gives 1 cup fresh puree

GINGER-GARLIC PASTE

For a good ginger-garlic paste, peel and chop 10 flakes of garlic and 1" piece of ginger. Grind together without any water or use the minimum amount of water, may be a few spoons, just enough to grind it. These paste are less in quantity, so you need a small spice grinder to grind these. You can put the paste in a small box and store in the refrigerator for 8-10 days.

I like to make ginger and garlic pastes separately and store them in separate boxes in the refrigerator. If the recipe needs 1 tsp of ginger-garlic paste, I use ½" piece of ginger and 3- 4 flakes of garlic.

Ginger-Garlic paste .... ready made or fresh?
Fresh is more flavourful, but when you do use ready made, add a little extra.

GARAM MASALA

Makes ¼ cup
5-6 sticks cinnamon (dalchini), each about 2" long
15-20 black cardamom pods (moti illaichi)
¾ tbsp cloves (laung)
2 tbsp black peppercorns (saboot kali mirch)
2 tbsp cumin seeds (jeera)
½ flower of mace (javitri)

1. Remove seeds of black cardamoms. Discard skin.
2. Roast all ingredients together in a non stick pan or kadhai for 2 minutes on low heat, stirring constantly till fragrant.
3. Remove from heat. Cool. Grind to a fine powder in a clean coffee or spice grinder. Store in a small jar with a tight fitting lid.

TANDOORI MASALA

Makes ½ cup
2 tbsp coriander seeds (saboot dhania)
2 tbsp cumin seeds (jeera)
1 tbsp fenugreek seeds (methi daana)
1 tbsp black peppercorns (saboot kali mirch)
1 tbsp cloves (laung)
seeds of 8 black cardamom pods (moti illaichi)
2 tsp paprika or degi mirch
1 tbsp dried fenugreek leaves (kasoori methi)
1 tbsp ground cinnamon (dalchini)
½ tbsp ground ginger (sonth)
½ tsp red chilli powder

1. In a non stick pan or kadhai, roast together — coriander seeds, cumin seeds, fenugreek seeds, black pepper corns, cloves and cardamom seeds, on moderate heat for about 1 minute, until fragrant.
2. Remove from heat and let the spices cool down. Grind to a fine powder. Transfer to a bowl and mix in the remaining ingredients. Store in an air tight jar.

SAMBHAR POWDER

Makes ½ cup
¼ cup coriander seeds (saboot dhania)
1 tbsp cumin seeds (jeera)
1 tbsp dried, split yellow chick peas (channe ki dal)
2 tsp fenugreek seeds (methi daana)
5-6 dry, red chillies (saboot lal mirch)
½ tsp asafoetida (hing)
1½ tsp peppercorns (saboot kali mirch)

1. Roast all ingredients together over low heat in a non stick pan or kadhai, until fragrant.
2. Cool the spices and grind to a fine powder in a small coffee grinder. Store in an air tight jar.

BASIC EGG RECIPES

BOILED EGG

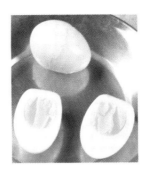

Serves 1

1 egg
salt and pepper - to taste
water - enough to immerse egg

1. Put enough water in a saucepan to cover the egg.
2. Bring the water to boil and lower the egg into the boiling water.
3. Let the egg boil on high heat. Allow 3 minutes for a half-boiled egg, 5-7 minutes for soft-boiled egg and 10-12 minutes for hard-boiled egg.
4. Remove boiled egg from saucepan. Cool the egg immediately under cold water to prevent discoloration.
5. Serve the half-boiled and the soft-boiled eggs in egg cups with salt and pepper. Hard boiled egg may be sliced or quartered as desired.

SCRAMBLED EGG

Serves 2

2 eggs
1 small onion - chopped
1 small tomato- chopped, 1 green chilli- chopped
¼ tsp each of salt and pepper
2 tbsp butter or oil

1. Lightly beat the eggs in a bowl with a fork. Add ¼ tsp salt and ¼ tsp pepper.
2. Heat butter or oil in a frying pan over moderate heat, add onion, cook till soft.
3. Pour all the egg mixture, green chilli and tomato. Stir continuously so that it does not stick to the bottom of the pan.
4. Cook for about 2-3 minutes until eggs are cooked. Add more salt and pepper if required. Serve hot garnished with parsley or coriander.

OMELETTE

Serves 2

2 eggs
1 small onion - chopped
1 small tomato- chopped, 1 green chilli- chopped
¼ tsp each of salt and pepper
2- 3 tbsp butter or oil

1. Beat eggs well in a bowl with a fork.
2. Add onion, tomato, green chilli, salt and pepper to the eggs in the bowl. Mix well.
3. Melt butter or oil in a frying pan (preferably nonstick) on a medium-low heat, tilting the pan to grease the sides and the bottom of the pan nicely.
4. Pour the eggs into the pan, tilt to spread the batter till the sides. Cook on medium heat till it sets and the under side is golden brown. With a spatula gently lift the egg pancake and turn immediately to cook the other side. Cook till golden on both the sides.
5. Slide on to a plate. Fold into half and serve hot with buttered toasts.

CHEESE & MUSHRROM OMELETTE

Cut 2-3 mushrooms into slices. Saute them in 2 tsp butter till soft. Stir in 2 tbsp grated cheddar cheese and remove from fire. Put this mixture on the omelette before folding it.

Mocktails/Drinks

Be imaginative and creative while preparing mocktails. Try combining different ready-made juices like pineapple, guava, grape, peach etc. with other drinks. To add tang to the drink, try adding some lime cordial or ginger ale (available ready-made) to the drink. Different juices and drinks may be blended for an interesting combination. Suggested combinations: pineapple and orange juice; apple and tomato juice; khus syrup and limca, coconut milk with pineapple juice etc. A little cream or ice cream, just 1 tsp per serving may be blended with the juice to give it a creamier texture. Remember to blend it nicely using a mixer/grinder.

LIME ICE TEA

A cool, economical and refreshing drink.

INGREDIENTS

Serves 3-4

BLACK TEA
1 cup water, 1½ tsp tea leaves

SUGAR SYRUP
2½ cups water, ½ cup sugar

OTHER INGREDIENTS
1 big bunch of mint leaves, chopped roughly along with stems
2 lemons, crushed ice and lemon slices to serve
fresh cherries or grapes

METHOD

1   Boil water. Remove from fire. Add tea leaves. Stir.
2   Pour this black tea over chopped mint leaves kept in a saucepan. Leave to cool.
3   Strain tea when it cools to room temperature. Keep aside.
4   Prepare sugar syrup by boiling water and sugar together. Remove from fire when sugar dissolves.
5   Mix tea and sugar syrup.
6   Remove the peel of the lemons as a strip for garnishing. Keep peel aside. Squeeze lemon juice into the tea mixture. Chill the ice tea.
7   Put a slice of lemon and a cherry in a tall glass. Add lots of ice. Pour the iced tea on top.
8   Serve garnished with a fruit stick. To make the stick, take out the peel of a lemon in a strip form with a sharp knife. Thread one end in a toothpick. Insert a mint leaf and then twist the lemon peel around the tooth pick and thread it again at the other end. Top with a cherry. Serve.

FRUIT PUNCH

INGREDIENTS

Serves 3-4

2 cups orange juice, 2 cups pineapple juice
2 tbsp fresh cream or ice cream
1-2 tbsp powdered sugar- optional, 8-10 ice cubes

GARNISH
strawberries or lemon slices or slices of fresh pineapple with the peel cut into triangular pieces

METHOD

1   Mix orange juice, pineapple juice and cream or ice cream with ice in a mixer/blender. Add sugar to taste. Pour in small thin glasses and serve garnished with a fruit inserted on the rim of the glass. Make a small slit in the fruit and push it down on the glass rim.

Readymade Tetra packs of cream...

It is a good idea to have small ready-made tetra packs of cream in the fridge. Unlike fresh cream from the dairies, it has a long shelf life when not opened. Once opened, the cream lasts for a week in the chill tray of the fridge. Remember to cut a small hole at the corner of the flap, so that the flap can be turned properly and the cream stays in good condition for long.

STARTERS & SNACKS

Snacks are taken in-between main meals. Starters are also snacks but served before the main meal as appetizers. So a starter should be light to eat, dainty to look at and also comfortable to hold. They are also called finger foods. Any snack which is not too filling, can be made smaller in size and served as a starter before the main meal.

CLUB SANDWICH

A three layered toasted sandwich.

INGREDIENTS

Serves 2-3

4 tbsp mayonnaise (ready made or see recipe on page 81)
1 small chicken breast - boiled & shredded (½ cup), see page 36
¼ cup finely shredded cabbage, ¼ cup grated carrot
¼ tsp pepper, ½ tsp mustard
1 egg omelette - see recipe on page 55
1 cheese slice
1 small cucumber - wash and slice along with the peel into paper thin slices
6 slices white or brown bread, some butter - enough to spread

METHOD

1   Mix mayonnaise, shredded chicken, cabbage, carrot, pepper and mustard sauce in a bowl. Mix well. Check seasonings. Add more if required.

2   Toast all the bread slices and spread some butter on one side of each bread. Place a cheese slice. Lay some cucumber slices on the cheese. Place another buttered toast on it, with the butter side down on the cucumber pieces.

3   Place omelette on bread. Spread some mayonnaise mixture on the last slice of bread and press on the omelette. Keep this sandwich aside.

4   Repeat with the other slices to make another sandwich.

5   Trim the edges of a sandwich and cut each sandwich diagonally into four pieces. Serve sandwich with french fries and tomato ketchup. To decorate the sandwich, pierce a small piece of lettuce or cabbage leaf through a tooth pick and top with a cherry.

Variation: For Veg Club Sandwich, add finely chopped capsicum instead of chicken and instead of egg omelette, use thin paneer slices sprinkled with salt and pepper. You can also use a thin vegetable cutlet instead of the omelette.

PERFECT FRENCH FRIES

Serves 2

INGREDIENTS

2-3 potatoes, 1 tsp of maida, oil for frying, ¼ tsp salt

METHOD

1   Peel 2-3 potatoes and cut into ¼" thick round slices. Stack the slices and cut them into ¼" broad strips or fingers.

2   Keep for about 10 minutes in cold water to which 1-2 tsp salt has been added.

3   Drain and wipe dry on a clean kitchen towel.

4   Sprinkle 1 tsp of maida on the potato fingers to absorb any water if present. Mix well with fingers.

5   Heat oil in a kadhai, about half kadhai full or slightly less than half full.

6   Add all the fingers and fry for 3-4 minutes till very light golden. Remove from oil on a paper napkin. Immediately sprinkle ¼ tsp salt.

7   Just before serving, reheat the oil and fry the chips quickly for 2 minutes until crisp and golden brown.

FISH FINGERS WITH TARTAR SAUCE

It is a good idea to make friends with the fish monger. You are sure to get fresh fish.

INGREDIENTS

Serves 6-8

½ kg firm white fish fillet (Sole), without bones - cut into fingers
1 tbsp lemon juice and 2 tbsp besan (gram flour)
1 cup dry bread crumbs for coating, see page 48

MARINADE
1 tbsp ginger garlic paste
2 tbsp lemon juice
1½ tsp salt, 1 tsp pepper powder, ½ tsp red chilli powder
2 eggs
4 tbsp cornflour

TARTAR SAUCE
½ cup readymade mayonnaise or see page 81
1 tbsp very finely chopped onion
1 tbsp very finely chopped cucumber (kheera)
2 tbsp brown vinegar

METHOD

1. Rub a little lemon juice and besan on the fish fingers. Keep aside for 30 minutes. Wash fish well. Transfer to a kitchen towel and pat till well dried.

2. To prepare the marinade, mix all the ingredients written under marinade in a bowl. Add fish and mix well. Keep aside for ½ hour.

3. Spread bread crumbs in a flat plate. Pick up one piece of marinated fish and coat over dry breadcrumbs. Coat and cover the fish completely with bread crumbs on all the sides. Spread fish fingers on a plate and cover with a plastic wrap. Keep in the fridge till serving time.

4. To prepare the tartar sauce, soak the onion and cucumber in vinegar for 10-15 minutes.

5. Strain the cucumber and onion in vinegar to drain out the vinegar. Press gently to remove any excess vinegar. Gently mix it into the mayonnaise. Keep tartar sauce in the fridge.

6. At serving time, heat oil in a pan. Reduce heat. Fry a few fish fingers on medium heat till golden. Do not fry on high heat otherwise the fish will brown quickly without getting cooked. Drain on paper napkins to absorb excess oil. Serve hot with tartar sauce.

TiP

Add some mustard powder and red chilli flakes and a pinch of salt to the bread crumbs to make it tastier.

The oil used for frying fish acquires a distinct taste and cannot be used for frying other foods. Try using less oil for frying fish and keep it separately after frying the fish.

To remove fishy odour from your hands, rub them with some toothpaste and wash hands well.

There are a few brands of mayonnaise available in the market that are really good. All you need to do is - add some flavourings (pepper, oregano, mustard paste etc.), thin down the mayo a little with some yogurt/curd and you have a saucy dip ready to serve.

AMRITSARI PANEER

A snack resembling our all time favourite paneer pakoras.

INGREDIENTS

Serves 4

250 gms paneer (buy a block of paneer weighing 250 gms)
12-15 flakes of garlic & 1½" piece of ginger - crushed to a paste
(2 tbsp ginger-garlic paste)
½ tsp ajwain (carom seeds)
a few drops of orange colour
½ tsp salt, ½ tsp pepper and red chilli powder
5-6 tbsp besan (gram flour), or more if required
oil for frying
ready-made chat masala to sprinkle on the paneer

METHOD

1 Cut paneer into thin long fingers.

2 Mix ginger-garlic paste, ajwain, colour, salt, pepper and red chilli powder in a bowl.

3 Add the paneer fingers, mix gently so that all the sides of paneer gets coated with the spices. Keep paneer aside till serving time.

4 At serving time, heat oil in a kadhai on medium flame.

5 Spread besan in a flat plate. Pick up one piece of paneer at a time and coat with the besan spread in the plate. Coat on all the sides. Repeat for all the paneer pieces. Add more besan if required.

6 Deep fry till crisp and golden brown. Drain on paper napkins. Serve generously sprinkled with chaat masala.

Is the oil ready for frying?

Put a tiny piece of bread in hot oil. If the oil sizzles and the bread turns golden within 30 seconds, and comes to the surface, go ahead and fry the paneer. Extra hot oil will turn the bread dark brown. If the oil is not hot enough, the bread will quietly remain at the bottom and it will absorb too much oil during browning.

Crispy Pakoras!

For crispy pakoras, make batter with ice cold water and fry them twice. Half fry them before and fry them again at serving time. However paneer pakoras should be fried only once because frying them a second time makes them tough. Also, adding a little oil to the batter makes crisp pakoras.

CHEESY CHICKEN TRIANGLES

Grilled bread slices smeared with mustard and topped with chicken & cheese.

INGREDIENTS

Serves 4

6-8 slices of white bread
1 boneless chicken breast (100 gms)
4 tbsp/50 gms grated cheddar cheese or processed cheese (use cubes or tin)
Some ready-made mustard paste or masala chilli tomato sauce - enough to spread
½ of a medium tomato - remove pulp (seed portion) and cut into tiny squares

SAUCE (1 cup)
  1 tbsp yellow butter
2 tbsp maida (flour)
½ of a medium capsicum - chopped finely
1 cup milk
½ tsp salt or to taste
¼ tsp freshly crushed peppercorns (saboot kali mirch) to taste
¼ cup ready-made cream

METHOD

1   Wash the chicken. Put chicken, ½ tsp salt & ½ cup water in a deep pan (patila). Cover and cook for 5-7 minutes or till tender. Alternately, pressure cook chicken with ½ cup water and ½ tsp salt to give 1 whistle and then keep on low heat for 2 minutes. Remove from fire. Remove the bones from the chicken meat and cut into very small cubes or pieces. (You get about ¾ cup of small chicken pieces).

2   To prepare the sauce, put butter in a heavy bottomed kadhai or a nonstick pan. Let it melt, do not burn. Add maida and stir with a spoon for a minute. Add capsicum. Mix. Remove from fire. Add milk, stirring continuously with the other hand. Return to fire and cook, stirring continuously till thick. Add salt and pepper. Remove from fire.

3   Add cream, boiled chicken and half of the cheese to the sauce. Check seasonings and add more if required. Keep chicken mixture aside.

4   Spread mustard paste or masala chilli tomato sauce on each slice of bread.

5   Spread 2 tbsp of the chicken mixture on each bread slice. Repeat with all the bread slices. Then sprinkle some grated cheese and a few tomato pieces and crushed peppercorns on each slice with chicken mixture. Repeat with all the bread slices. Keep the slices on the wire rack of the oven.

6   Grill in a hot oven for 7-8 minutes or till slightly brown. Remove from oven and cut diagonally from the centre to get 2 triangular pieces. Serve immediately.

Note: If you do not have masala chilli tomato sauce, mix 2 tsp of red chilli sauce with 2 tbsp tomato sauce.

Handling White Sauce

Stirring plays a very important role in getting a smooth, lump free white sauce. When adding milk to the flour mix, stir vigorously with the other hand. There is a wonderful wire/balloon whisk that makes this task so much simpler.

PANEER TIKKA

You can marinate the paneer in the marinade and keep in the fridge for a day. It saves a lot of botheration on the day of the party.

INGREDIENTS

Serves 4

300 gm paneer - cut into 1½" pieces of 1" thickness
1 large capsicum - deseeded and cut into 1" pieces (12 pieces)
1 onion - cut into 4 pieces and then separated

MARINADE
½ cup dahi (yogurt) - hang in a muslin cloth for 15 minutes
3 tbsp thick malai or thick cream
1" piece ginger, 5-6 flakes garlic - crushed to a paste (2 tsp ginger - garlic paste)
a few drops of orange colour or a pinch of haldi (turmeric)
1½ tbsp oil, 1 tbsp (level) cornflour
½ tsp amchoor, ¾ tsp salt, or to taste, ½ tsp chaat masala
1 tbsp tandoori masala or ¾ tsp garam masala

Never make thin paneer tikkas.

The paneer pieces should be atleast ½-1" thick. Thin pieces tend to get hard after cooking. If you ever feel that the paneer might run short, make big tikkas and cut them into 2 pieces at serving time.

METHOD

1 Hang yogurt in a muslin cloth (mal-mal ka kapda) for 15 minutes.

2 Transfer the hung yogurt to a flat bowl. Beat till smooth.

3 Add 1½ tbsp oil, 1 tbsp cornflour, amchoor, salt, chaat masala, tandoori masala, colour or haldi to the paste.

4 Add ginger-garlic paste & cream or malai to the marinade. Mix well.

5 Add paneer to the marinade. Mix well so that all pieces of paneer get well coated with the marinade on all the sides.

6 Grease the wire rack of the oven well with oil. Arrange paneer on the greased rack. After arranging all the paneer pieces on the wire rack, put the capsicum and onions - both together in the left over marinade in which paneer was kept. Mix well to coat the vegetables with the marinade. Leave the vegetables in the bowl itself.

7 About ½ hour before serving, put the paneer pieces placed on the wire rack in the hot oven at about 180°C. Bake/grill for 15 minutes or till almost done. Bake/grill the paneer till it gets slightly dry.

8 Brush the pieces with 2 tbsp of melted butter or sprinkle some oil on the paneer pieces (basting). Now remove the vegetables from the bowl and put them also in the oven on the sides of the paneer. Grill/bake everything together for another 10 minutes. The vegetables should not be in the oven for too long.

9 Remove from the oven. Transfer to a serving platter. If you like microwave for 1 minute to further soften the paneer. Serve immediately (really hot), sprinkled with some lemon juice and chaat masala with dahi poodina chutney given on page 73.

Preventing Paneer From Hardening

Paneer Tikkas should not be cooked in the oven for too long, thinking that they will turn nice and crisp. On the contrary, paneer will turn hard and chewy. Serve immediately as on keeping it turns hard.

Also, do not forget to baste them with butter in between, when half done.

CHICKEN ROLLS

Crisp from outside and soft from inside. Always better to make them atleast 1 hour before serving as they hold their shape better on keeping in the fridge for sometime.

INGREDIENTS

Makes 6

300 gm chicken with bones - cut into 3-4 pieces
1 tbsp chopped green coriander
1 small onion - chopped
4 tbsp butter
3 tbsp maida (flour)
½ cup milk
¾ tsp salt, ½ tsp pepper to taste, ½ tsp red chilli powder
COATING
1 egg white, ½ cup bread crumbs

METHOD

1   Heat 4 tbsp butter in a kadhai or pan. Add chicken pieces, stir fry on medium heat for 4-5 minutes. Reduce heat to medium, cover and cook for 4- 5 minutes. Remove chicken from the kadhai. Let it cool. Remove bones from the chicken. Shred into very small pieces.

2   To the same kadhai or pan, add chopped onion. Cook for 1-2 minutes or till onion turns soft.

3   Add coriander and saute for 1 minute. Add 3 tbsp maida, stir for 1 minute on low heat. Remove from fire.

4   Remove from heat and gradually add the milk, stirring continuously with the other hand so as not to form lumps. If lumps do appear, press them against the sides of the pan to dissolve them.

5   Put the kadhai or pan back on fire. Add salt and pepper and ½ tsp red chilli powder. Cook till the sauce turns very thick like a solid and starts leaving the sides of the pan.

6   Remove from heat. Add shredded chicken. Mix well. Cool.

7   Shape the mixture into 6 rolls, with wet hands. Flatten the sides by pressing sides on a flat surface.

8   Beat egg white in a wide bowl. Spread bread crumbs in flat plate. Coat each roll in egg white and then roll over dry bread crumbs. Keep aside in the fridge till serving time.

9   To serve, take out the rolls from fridge, keep aside.

10 Heat oil in a kadhai for deep frying the roll. Add rolls one at a time and deep fry on a medium heat to a golden colour. Serve hot with ketchup.

Breading

Any time you coat something with crumbs, the crumbs will stick better if you give the item a little chilling time in the fridge.

Instant Bread Crumbs

To get dry bread crumbs instantly, tear 2-3 pieces of bread into small pieces. Place on a micro proof plate and microwave for 2 minutes. Mix them with the fingers and microwave again for a minute. Keep aside for 5 minutes to dry out. Grind in a mixer to get instant dry crumbs.

PAO BHAJI

This delicious bhaji served with hot buns, is really relishing.

INGREDIENTS

ervings 7-8

IGREDIENTS

 flower of a medium cauliflower (phoolgobhi) - chopped (1½ cups)
 flower of cabbage (bandgobhi) - chopped (1½ cups)
-5 tbsp oil
 onions - finely chopped, 1 cup shelled peas (matar)
 potatoes - boiled & mashed roughly
 tbsp Pao-Bhaji Masala, 1½ tsp salt, or to taste
 tomatoes - finely chopped
0 gms butter (4 tbsp), 1 tbsp chopped coriander

RIND TO A PASTE

" piece ginger, 4-6 flakes garlic - optional, 2-4 green chillies

AO (BUNS) TO SERVE

METHOD

1 Put cauliflower and cabbage with ½ cup water in a pressure cooker. Pressure cook to give one whistle. Keep on low flame for 5 minutes. Remove from fire.

2 Grind ginger, garlic and green chillies to a paste.

3 Heat 4- 5 tbsp oil in a kadhai. Add chopped onions and cook till onions turn light golden.

4 Add peas and cook covered till tender.

5 Add prepared ginger paste and cook for 2-3 minutes on low flame.

6 Add pao-bhaji masala and salt. Stir for a minute.

7 Add tomatoes and cook covered for 5-6 minutes, stirring in between. Mash them well with a kadchhi so that the tomatoes blend well with the masala.

8 Add pressure cooked vegetables and potatoes. Cook for 5-7 minutes, mashing them continuously.

9 Add 4 tbsp butter and chopped coriander. Keep aside.

10 To serve, cut buns into halves. Heat 1-2 tbsp butter in a pan or tawa and press the buns on the butter to make them turn golden and soft.

11 Serve onions mixed in dahi poodina chutney (page 73) along with the hot pao-bhaji.

CLASSIC VEGETARIAN PIZZA

Forget the expensive restaurant pizza and enjoy this home made one! The toppings can be changed according to your liking. Extra cheese may be added for a melting cheesy pizza.

INGREDIENTS

Serves 4-6

2 ready-made pizza bases
100-150 gms mozzarella or pizza cheese - grated (1-1½ cups)

TOMATO SPREAD
2 tbsp oil
6-8 flakes of garlic - crushed to a paste
¼ cup ready made tomato puree
2 tbsp tomato ketchup
1 tsp oregano (dried), ½ tsp salt and ¼ tsp pepper

CLASSIC TOPPING
½ cup tinned sweet corn kernels or 50 gm baby corns - cut into half lengthwise
3-4 mushrooms - cut into paper thin slices
1 onion - cut into ½ and then into semi circles or half rings
½ red and ½ green capsicum - cut into ½" pieces
a few black or green olives - sliced
1 firm tomato - cut into 4 pieces, desseded and cut into ½" pieces
salt and freshly ground peppercorns to taste

METHOD

1 To prepare the tomato spread, heat oil. Add garlic. Stir and add tomato puree, tomato sauce, oregano, salt and pepper. Cook for 3-4 minutes on medium heat or till oil separates. Remove from heat.

2 Spread tomato spread on each pizza base, leaving the edges.

3 Sprinkle more than half of the cheese on both the bases (reserve a little for the top).

4 Spread capsicum and onions. Sprinkle some salt and pepper. Sprinkle mushrooms and corn.

5 Arrange olives and slices of tomato. Sprinkle the remaining cheese. Sprinkle some oregano too.

6 Grease the wire rack of the oven. Put pizza on the wire rack. Place the pizza in the hot oven. Bake at 200°C for 10-12 minutes or till the base gets crisp and the cheese melts. To get a pan crisp pizza, oil the base a little before baking.

7 Serve hot with chilli flakes and mustard sauce.

Why is pizza placed on the rack and not on the tray when put in the oven?

When pizza is placed on a tray, the bottom of the tray stops the heat from reaching the bottom of the pizza base. On the other hand, the pizza placed on the wire or grill rack gets enough heat from the space in between the wires, making the pizza crisp. So a rack is good for pizzas, tikkas, bread snacks etc., where you want the base to be crisp.

Mozzarella or Cheddar

Mozzarella cheese melts and forms cheesy strings when cooked. It is the ideal cheese for topping pizzas. Cheddar is a tasty, mature cheese, which does not melt on cooking. Added to sauces, it enhances the flavour greatly.

TIP

Never add garlic to very hot oil, it will turn brown and lose most of its flavour.

69

RAWA IDLIS

Suji idlis made instantly. Buy coarse suji available in packets. Fine suji will not give perfect idlis.

INGREDIENTS

Serves 8

1 cup suji (rawa), coarse semolina
1½ tbsp oil
1 cup curd (dahi)
½ tsp soda-bi-carb (mitha soda)
¾ tsp salt, ½ cup water, approx.
a few curry leaves

METHOD

1 Heat 1½ tbsp oil in a kadhai. Add suji and mix well. Stir on low heat for 2 minutes till it just starts to change colour. Remove from fire. Add salt. Mix well. Keep aside to cool.

2 Add curd to the suji mixture. Mix well with a spoon or a wire whisk.

3 Add soda-bi-carb. Mix very well till smooth. Keep the batter aside for 10 minutes.

4 Take an idli mould and put 1- 2 drops of oil in each round cup and spread it evenly with your fingers. Put 2 tbsp batter in each cup and put a split cashewnut or curry leaf in each cup.

5 Put a big deep pan filled with 1" high water on fire, to boil. After the water boils, reduce heat.

6 Place the idli mould into the pan of water. Increase heat to medium. Cover the pan with a lid. Steam for 14-15 minutes undisturbed on medium flame. Insert a knife in the idli, if it comes out clean it's done. Remove from fire.

7 Remove the idlis from the mould after 5 minutes with the help of a knife. Keep idlis covered in a casserole till serving time.

8 To serve, steam them again by placing them in the mould and putting the mould back in the deep pan with a little water. Steam for 3-4 minutes till heated properly. Serve hot with coconut chutney and sambhar given on page 120.

COCONUT CHUTNEY

INGREDIENTS

Serves 8

CHUTNEY

½ cup freshly grated or desiccated coconut powder (nariyal ka bura)
¼ cup roasted channa or channe ki dal (split gram) - roasted
1 green chilli - chopped, 1 onion - chopped
¾ tsp salt, ¼" piece ginger
1 cup sour curd (khatti dahi)- approx.

BAGHAR (TADKA)

1 tbsp oil
1 tsp sarson (mustard seeds)
1-2 dry red chillies - broken into small pieces, a few curry leaves

METHOD

1 Grind all ingredients of the chutney in a mixer grinder, adding enough curd to get the right consistency. Keep aside in a bowl.

2 Heat 1 tbsp oil in a small kadhai or pan, add sarson. Wait for ½ a minute, add broken red chillies.

3 Remove from fire, pout the baghar immediately into the chutney, mix well. Serve with idlis.

Steaming Idlis

The preferred way to steam idlis or any vegetable is to steam it on medium high heat. Do not keep the heat low otherwise the water does not boil properly and enough steam is not formed, leaving the idlis undercooked.

BEAN BITES

A very simple starter. Biscuits are topped with beans, sour cream and crunchy peanuts.

INGREDIENTS

Serves 8

1 packet cream cracker biscuits
or
any other salted biscuits like monacco

BEAN TOPPING
¾ cup of ready-made baked beans (tin)
1 tbsp yellow butter
1 tbsp chopped coriander or parsley
2 flakes of garlic
¼ tsp salt, ¼ tsp pepper to taste
1- 2 drops of tabasco sauce (optional)

SOUR CREAM
½ cup thick curd (dahi)
¼ tsp salt
¼ tsp freshly crushed pepper (saboot kali mirch, powdered)
1 green chilli - remove seeds and chop finely

CRUNCHY GARNISH
2 tbsp chopped coriander or 1 spring onion- chop green part very finely
2 tbsp roasted peanuts (moongphali) - crushed coarsely

METHOD

1 To prepare the sour cream, hang curd in a muslin cloth for 20 minutes.

2 Beat the hung curd with a wire whisk or fork till smooth. Add salt and pepper to taste. Mix in very finely chopped green chillies. Keep aside.

3 For bean topping, put butter in a kadhai, let it melt a little, add garlic and fry till it starts to change colour.

4 Add ready-made beans, coriander, salt and pepper. Cook for 2 minutes. Remove from fire. Add tabasco if using. Keep aside.

5 At serving time, heat the filling and spread 1 heaped teaspoon of it on each cream cracker, leaving the edges clean.

6 Drop ½ tsp of the sour cream in the centre portion. Sprinkle some greens of the spring onion on the sour cream. Put a few crushed peanuts. Serve immediately.

Keep peanuts in the fridge, they will last much longer! Outside they might acquire a fowl smell and taste. Actually all nuts keep best in the fridge.

HOW TO?

Transfer the left over baked beans to a steel or plastic container/box. Keep it in freezer compartment of the refrigerator for 1-2 months, and use as required.

TiP
½ cup boiled rajmah mixed with ¼ cup tomato sauce and ¼ tsp each of oregano, salt and pepper can be used instead of the ready made baked beans.

Chutneys & Dips

Dahi Poodina Chutney

Goes very well with Indian snacks and tandoori food. It is delicious with the main meal too.

INGREDIENTS

Serves 6

GRIND TOGETHER
2 cup poodina (mint), ½ cup hara dhania (green coriander)
2 green chillies, ½ of a medium onion, 2 flakes garlic
1 pinch of kala namak, ¼ tsp bhuna jeera (roasted cumin), salt to taste

ADD LATER
½ cups curd - hang for 15 minutes in a muslin cloth
1 tsp oil, 1 tsp lemon juice
2 tbsp cream or milk (optional)

METHOD

1. Hang curd for 15 minutes in a thin muslin cloth (mal- mal ka kapda).
2. Wash coriander and mint leaves. Grind together coriander, mint, green chillies, onion, garlic, kala namak, bhuna jeera, salt with 2-3 tbsp water to a paste in a mixer grinder.
3. Beat hung curd well till smooth with a wire or baloon whisk or fork. Transfer to a bowl.
4. To hung curd, add enough green paste to get a nice light green colour.
5. Add lemon juice and oil. If the chutney appears thick, add some milk or cream.

Cheesy Dip

Goes very well with snacks like rolls, cutlets & potato wafers.

INGREDIENTS

4 tbsp cheese spread
½ cup curd- hang in a muslin cloth for 15 minutes
½ tsp oregano, ½ tsp salt, ½ tsp black pepper
1 tsp lemon juice, ¼ tsp red chilli flakes, 1 tsp tomato ketchup
3 tbsp milk, approx.

METHOD

1. Mix all ingredients together in a mixing bowl with a wire whisk, to get a dip with a coating consistency. It should not be too runny nor very thick.

One Minute Cheesy Dip Accompaniment

Cut peeled carrots, unpeeled cucumber, peeled fresh pineapple slices, unpeeled round apple slices into thin fingers. Put in a small glass half filled with ice cubes and serve with the above cheesy dip. It serves as a good fill-in-the-blank while the main starters are being fried or grilled.

Soups

These light soups will be wonderful as appetizers before a formal meal. Here are some ideas to add flavour and garnish it to give that special touch. You can even do these tricks with the ready-made soup packets and give them a home made fresh taste. I bet nobody will know it's a readymade one!

Seasoning Cubes... What are they?

These are small packets of a special powder which is full of flavour. It can be mixed in water and used as stock for any soup or sauces. Add 1-2 cubes to 2-4 cups of soup for great flavour. It has a lot of salt, so add salt only after tasting the soup.

Add Flavour and Garnish to Soups...

1 Add some lemon leaves to the boiling soup for a fragrant flavour. In the absence of lemon leaves, grate a whole lemon gently on the grater to get lemon rind which can be used instead of lemon leaves.

2 Tear some basil leaves and add towards the end of the cooking time. Basil goes well with tomato based soups.

3 Top soup bowls with grated cheese. It goes well with cream soups.

4 Thinly sliced slivers of toasted almond add to the eye appeal as well as the crunch.

5 Cream dropped with a spoon in a swirl over a bowl of soup is the evergreen garnish.

6 Very finely chopped coloured peppers (capsicums) just a spoon, makes all the difference when used as a topping for a cup of soup.

A Quick Accompaniment to Soups...

GARLIC BREAD

INGREDIENTS

Serves 8

1 French loaf

GARLIC SPREAD
6 tbsp olive oil or butter - softened
2-4 crushed flakes of garlic
a pinch salt, ¼ tsp pepper, ½ tsp red chilli flakes
½ tsp oregano

METHOD

1 Cut the loaf into ½" thick slices.

2 To prepare the spread, mix all the ingredients of spread in a small bowl.

3 Put the garlic spread on all the pieces of the bread.

4 To serve, bake in a preheated oven at 200°C for 15-20 minutes or till the bread turns crisp.

SWEET CORN VEGETABLE SOUP

INGREDIENTS

Serves 6-8

1 cream style sweet corn tin (460 gm), about 2½ cups
¼ cup carrot - finely chopped, ¼ cup cabbage - finely chopped
1 spring onion - finely chopped along with the greens
2-3 french beans - finely chopped
2 tbsp green chilli sauce, 1 tbsp red chill sauce
1 tbsp vinegar, ¼ tsp pepper, 2 tsp level salt
5 tbsp cornflour dissolved in ¾ cup water

Fresh Corn Soup

For fresh corns, grate 5 large corns and pressure cook grated corn with 9 cups water to give 1 whistle. Keep on low heat for 5 minutes. Remove from heat and let it cool down. Proceed from step 3.

METHOD

1. Dissolve cream style corn in 9 cups water in a deep pan. Bring to a boil. Boil for 5 minutes.
2. Add chilli sauces and vinegar. Simmer for 1-2 minutes.
3. Meanwhile heat 1 tbsp oil in a nonstick pan add the vegetables. Saute for 1 minute. Add the sauteed vegetables to the simmering soup. Simmer for 1 minute.
4. Add salt and pepper to the soup.
5. Add cornflour paste and cook for 2-3 minutes till the soup thickens. Serve hot.

CHICKEN SWEET CORN SOUP

INGREDIENTS

Serves 6

200 gm chicken with bones - cut into 3-4 pieces
1 tin sweet corn (cream style, 460 gm) (2½ cups)
1 spring onion - chopped alongwith the greens, keep greens separate
2 tbsp green chilli sauce, 1 tbsp red chill sauce
1 tbsp vinegar, ½ tsp ajinomoto (optional)
1 tsp salt, ¼ tsp pepper or to taste, 4 tbsp cornflour, 2 eggs - beaten lightly

METHOD

1. Put 9 cups water, chicken and 1 tsp salt in a pressure cooker. Pressure cook for 2 whistles and cook on low heat for another 2- 3 minutes. Remove from fire. Let the pressure drop by itself. Pick up the chicken pieces from the stock with the help of tongs (chimta). Let the stock remain in the cooker. Debone the meat from the chicken. Keep water (stock) in the pressure cooker aside.
2. Heat 2 tbsp oil separately in a pan. Add white of onions and chicken shreds and stir fry for 1 minute. Remove from fire.
3. Put the stock in the pressure cooker on fire, add sweet corn to stock and allow to boil on high heat for 5-7 minutes.
4. Add stir fried chicken to the simmering soup.
5. Add green chilli sauce, red chilli sauce, vinegar, ajinomoto, salt, pepper and green of spring onions to the soup in the cooker. Simmer for 1 minute.
6. Mix cornflour in ½ cup water, add to soup stirring constantly until soup is thick.
7. Beat eggs in a small bowl with a fork. Add the beaten eggs gradually, stirring soup immediately with a fork in the other hand, so that threads are formed.
8. Remove from fire. Serve hot in individual soup bowls along with soya sauce and green chillies in vinegar.

ORIENT VEGETABLE-NOODLE SOUP

A spicy, hot, clear soup with lots of vegetables. Lemon rind and tomato puree add a delicious flavour to this appetizer soup.

INGREDIENTS

Serves 4

1½ tbsp oil
4 mushrooms - sliced and then cut into thin long pieces
1 small carrot - grated
½ capsicum - finely chopped
10-12 spinach leaves - shredded or cut into thin strips
3 flakes garlic - chopped & crushed
2 whole, dried red chillies - deseed & cut into small pieces with a knife
30 gms noodles (½ cup) - break into 2" pieces
rind of 1 lemon
2 tsp green chilli sauce
¼ tsp pepper, 1¼ tsp salt
3 tbsp ready-made tomato puree
1½ tbsp vinegar, 1 tsp soya sauce

METHOD

1   Cut mushrooms into slices and cut each slice into thin long pieces.
2   To take out lemon rind, grate a firm whole lemon on the medium holes of the grater without applying too much pressure. Grate only the upper yellow skin without grating the white bitter pith beneath the yellow skin. Keep rind aside.
3   Heat oil in a pan. Reduce heat and add garlic. Saute briefly for ½ minute.
4   Add mushrooms, carrot and capsicum. Stir fry for 1 minute.
5   Add tomato puree and red chillies. Stir for ½ minute.
6   Add 4 cups of water. Bring the soup to a boil.
7   Add the noodles. Boil on medium heat for 2-3 minutes till noodles are soft.
8   Add salt, pepper, lemon rind, chilli sauce, soya sauce and vinegar.
9   Add the shredded spinach, simmer for 1 minute. Serve hot in soup bowls.

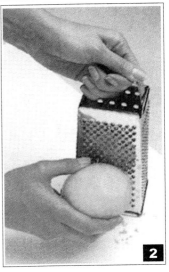

Note: This is a thin soup, but if you desire a slightly thick soup, add 1 tbsp cornflour dissolved in a little water to the boiling soup. Cook for 1-2 minutes till the soup thickens slightly. Serve hot.

How much Soya Sauce to add?

Soya sauce becomes darker in colour and concentrated on keeping. If you have an old bottle of soya sauce lying around, use sparingly and watch the colour of the soup. More can be added later according to the desired colour.

CREAM OF MUSHROOM

Most of the mushrooms are pureed to give taste and texture to the soup but some are finely chopped and added towards the end for that special bite. Garnished with some greens, it's a treat for the mushroom lovers.

INGREDIENTS

Serves 4-5

200 gm mushrooms
2 tsp butter, 1 onion - chopped
2 flakes garlic - crushed, 1 bay leaf (tej patta)
2 tbsp maida (plain flour)
1½ cups milk
1 tsp salt, ½ tsp white pepper
GARNISH
2 tbsp cream, some chopped spring onion greens (optional)

TiP

Always let the soup mixture cool down to room temperature before pureeing in the mixer. If you blend hot mixture steam gets formed, pushing open the cover of the mixer, and you end up spoiling the walls as well as your clothes

METHOD

1 Roughly chop 150 gm of mushrooms. Finely chop the remaining 50 gm of mushrooms for topping and keep aside.

2 Melt butter in a heavy bottom pan. Add chopped onion, 150 gm roughly chopped mushrooms, garlic and bay leaf. Stir for 3-4 minutes. Do not brown the onions.

3 Add maida and stir for 1 minute. Add 3 cups of water, 1 tsp salt, ½ tsp pepper and bring to a boil. Reduce heat and cook covered for 5 minutes. Remove from heat. Cool.

4 Place the cooled mixture in mixer and blend to a smooth puree. Strain the puree through a soup strainer (chhanni).

5 Put the puree back in the pan. Add milk and finely chopped mushrooms. Simmer for 2 minutes.

6 Lower heat and add cream and chopped spring onion. Mix well and serve hot.

CREAM OF TOMATO SOUP

You must have prepared tomato soup earlier but this tomato soup is really special! Once you give it a try, I bet you'll never go back to any other recipe.

INGREDIENTS

Serves 8

kg red tomatoes (must choose bright red ones)
carrot - chopped
onion - chopped
potato - chopped
-5 laung (cloves)
-5 saboot kali mirch (pepper corns)
" stick of dalchini (cinnamon)
tbsp butter
tsp salt
-2 tbsp sugar
tbsp cornflour

GARNISHING
slice of one day old bread - for croutons (see below)
w coriander leaves
tbsp cream, optional

METHOD

1 Heat butter in a pressure cooker. Add onion, carrot, potato, laung, saboot kali mirch and dalchini. Cook until onion turns pale and transparent.

2 Add washed whole tomatoes.

3 Add 6 cups water and pressure cook until two whistles. Keep on low heat for 2 minutes. Remove from fire.

4 Mash the tomatoes slightly and strain.

5 Keeping the liquid aside, churn the solid, unstrained part in the strainer in a mixer till smooth.

6 Strain again into the soup. Discard the solid residue this time.

7 Keep the soup on fire. Boil, stirring occasionally.

8 Add 3 tbsp cornflour dissolved in ½ cup of water.

9 Add salt, pepper and sugar and cook for 5-7 minutes.

10 To serve, pour hot soup in soup bowls. With a teaspoon put dots of cream on the soup and run a knife through the dots to get a feather effect. Serve hot.

Herbed Croutons

Cut one day old bread (old bread cuts better) into small pieces. Heat 2 tbsp butter or olive oil in a nonstick pan. Add 1 flake crushed garlic, 1 tbsp chopped fresh parsley or ½ tsp dried oregano or mixed herbs and bread. Stir for 4-5 minutes on medium heat till golden on all sides.

SALAD DRESSINGS

Dressings add colour, flavour, improve palatability and appearance of salads and are a means of combining ingredients. There are three general types of salad dressings from which many variations can be made.

Mayonnaise: A stable emulsion of oil and eggs.

French Dressing: A temporary emulsion of oil and acid like lemon juice or vinegar.

Cream Dressing: A semi stable emulsion of oil and cream.

MAYONNAISE

INGREDIENTS

Makes 1½ cups

2 eggs, 1½ cups oil
½ tsp salt, ½ tsp pepper, 1 tsp mustard powder
1 tsp sugar, 1 tbsp vinegar, 1 tbsp lemon juice

METHOD

1 Break eggs into the blender of your mixer. Add salt, pepper, sugar, mustard and vinegar to the eggs. Churn for a few seconds to blend all ingredients.

2 Keeping the blender on, add oil slowly spoonful by spoonful, churning all the time.

3 Keep adding oil gradually, till the sauce starts to thicken. Once the sauce thickens slightly, keeping the blender on, pour the oil in a thin stream from the cup directly in larger quantities. Churn till all the oil is used up and you get a thick mayonnaise dressing.

4 Add lemon juice. Churn once more. Remove from mixer to a bowl. Chill for 2 hours before use.

FRENCH DRESSING

INGREDIENTS

Makes ¼ cup

2 tbsp vinegar, ½ cup olive oil or any cooking oil
½ tsp French mustard or mustard powder
1 tsp salt, ½ tsp powdered sugar, ½ tsp pepper powder
2 tsp lemon juice

METHOD

1 Put all ingredients in a bottle with a tight fitting lid. Shake vigorously. Refrigerate until needed. Shake again before use.

Note: Excess French dressing will make green leafy vegetables flabby.

CREAM DRESSING

INGREDIENTS

Makes 1½ cups

1 cup cream - lightly beaten
½ cup olive oil, 2 tbsp vinegar
1 tsp mustard
½ tsp salt, ¼ tsp sugar
¼ tsp black pepper, ¼ tsp red chilli powder
1 tsp sesame seeds (til) - toasted

METHOD

1 Place all the ingredients in a bottle and shake well.

Note: Tastes good with broccoli and mushroom salad.

Interesting Variations:
Any one of these may be added to the above dressings:
2-3 flakes crushed garlic; 1-2 tsp tomato sauce; ½ tsp of dried mixed herbs; toasted & chopped almonds; orange juice; honey; lemon rind; fresh herbs like 1 tsp crushed mint etc.

RUSSIAN SALAD

Chicken and pineapple tid-bits go well together. For vegetarians, omit chicken and add 1 potato, cut into small pieces and boiled in salted water. You can add some paneer cubes too if you like.

INGREDIENTS

Serves 4-6

300 gms chicken with bones or 1 potato
1 tbsp vinegar, 1 tbsp oil
½ cup peas (matar)
2 carrots - diced neatly into small cubes (1½ cups)
8-10 french beans - chopped (½ cup)
½ capsicum - cut into thin long pieces (juliennes)
4-5 slices of pineapple (tinned), salt and pepper to taste
a few crisp lettuce leaves - chill in a bowl of water for 2 hours to turn crisp

DRESSING
¾ cup ready made or home made mayonnaise, recipe on page 81
¼ cup fresh cream, 1 cube cheese - grated (4 tbsp) or 1 tbsp cheese spread
½ tsp salt, ½ tsp pepper

METHOD

1   To boil chicken, put it with ½ cup water and ½ tsp salt in a pressure cooker. Pressure cook to give 1 whistle and simmer on low heat for 3-4 minutes. Remove from fire. Remove meat from bones and cut into small pieces. Put in a bowl and sprinkle 1 tbsp vinegar and 1 tbsp oil on it. Keep aside for 15 minutes.
    If using potatoes, peel and cut potato into ½" pieces and boil in salted water till a knife inserted in it goes down smoothly. Drain, pat dry potatoes with a kitchen towel. Marinate them with oil and vinegar too.

2   Boil 2 cups water with ½ tsp salt. Add peas. As soon as the boil returns, keep boiling for 2 minutes till peas are tender. Add the beans and carrots and boil further for 1 minute. Remove from fire and strain. Add fresh water and strain again. Keep vegetables aside.

3   Prepare mayonnaise as given on the page 81, or you may buy ready-made also. Mix mayonnaise, cream, cheese spread, salt and pepper. Mix well.

4   Squeeze pineapple slices well to remove excess syrup. Chop finely.

5   Add shredded chicken or potato, chopped pineapple, boiled vegetables and capsicum to the mayonnaise. Mix well.

6   Taste and adjust seasonings if needed. Add more pepper if required. Keep aside till serving time.

7   To serve, add a little milk to the salad if it appears thick. Arrange lettuce on a flat or a shallow serving platter. Pile the salad in the platter, forming a pyramid (heap). Serve chilled.

Home made Mayo giving Problems...
If mayonnaise does not thicken or it curdles, remove from blender into a cup. Chill the curdled mixture for 5-7 minutes in the freezer. Break another egg into the empty blender. Churn. Keeping the blender on, add the old, curdled mayonnaise from the cup, spoon by spoon, into the blender. Keep adding the old mayonnaise till all is used & a new perfect mayonnaise is ready. Adjust seasonings.

JULIENNE CHICKEN SALAD

Everything is cut into thin, long juliennes (match sticks) and mixed with a mustard flavoured dressing.

INGREDIENTS

Serves 4-6

2 chicken breasts - boneless or 300 gms chicken sausages
6 baby corns
100 gm mushrooms
½ green capsicum, ½ yellow capsicum or 1 green capsicum
1 firm tomato

DRESSING
6 tbsp oil, preferably olive oil
2 tbsp vinegar
¼ tsp salt, ½ tsp pepper, ½ tsp powdered sugar
1 tsp mustard paste
1 tbsp chopped parsley (optional)
2-3 flakes garlic - crushed & chopped finely

METHOD

1 To boil chicken breast, put them with ½ cup water and ½ tsp salt in a pressure cooker. Pressure cook to give 1 whistle and simmer on low heat for 3-4 minutes. Remove from fire. Cut the breasts into thin strips to give juliennes. If using sausages, cut each into slanting pieces of about ¼" thickness.

2 Boil 2 cups water with 1 tsp salt and few drops of lemon juice. Add whole baby corns and mushrooms to boiling water. Boil for 2 minutes. Strain. Pat dry and cut baby corns diagonally into slices. Cut each mushroom into four pieces, lengthwise.

3 Heat 1 tbsp oil in a pan. Saute chicken or chicken sausages for 1 minute.

4 Deseed capsicum and cut into strips. Remove the pulp of the tomato and cut into thin strips.

5 Mix chicken, mushrooms, baby corns, capsicum and tomato in a salad bowl.

6 Mix all the ingredients of the dressing in an empty bottle with a screw cap. Shake well.

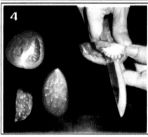

7 Pour the dressing over the salad and toss. Keep in the fridge.

8 Serve cold on a bed of lettuce leaves.

SOUR CREAM SALAD

A low cal creamy salad prepared from yogurt. Roasted peanuts add a delightful crunch to the salad.

INGREDIENTS

Serves 4

SOUR CREAM DRESSING
1 cup thick curd - hang for 30 minutes in a muslin cloth
2-3 tbsp grated cheese, cheddar or 1¼ tbsp cheese spread
75 gm (½ cup) fresh cream
2 tbsp roasted peanuts - split into halves or pounded
2 flakes garlic - crushed to a paste
1 tbsp olive oil
½ tsp oregano, 1 tsp tomato ketchup, ¾ tsp salt, ¼ tsp pepper

OTHER INGREDIENTS
¾ cup carrots - cut into ¼" pieces
½ cup sliced baby corns (round slices)
¼ cup chopped french beans
2 tbsp chopped celery stalks
½ cup finely chopped cucumber or capsicum
½ apple - chopped without peeling, or ½ cup grapes - halved
or 3 slices tinned pineapple - chopped into small pieces
a few lettuce or cabbage leaves - torn into 1" pieces

GARNISH
some musambi or red or green capsicum rings - cut into half
a tomato rose and parsley bunch

METHOD

1 Mix all ingredients of the sour cream dressing with a wire whisk or a balloon whisk till smooth. Do not mix in a mixer/blender.

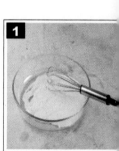

2 Boil 4-5 cups of water with 1 tsp salt and 1 tsp sugar. Add french beans, carrots and baby corns in boiling water and cook for 1-2 minutes till the vegetables are just done. Do not over cook.

3 When done, drain immediately and refresh by putting in cold water (so as to retain their colour). Strain. Keep in the strainer for 10 minutes for all the water to drain out.

4 Mix all vegetables and fruit in a large bowl.

5 Add the prepared dressing gradually over the fruit and vegetable mixture, mixing lightly. Check salt and pepper. Transfer to the serving dish.

6 Make a border of capsicum or musambi slices and make a tomato rose in the centre as shown on page 16. Arrange sprigs of parsley on the side of the rose. Serve cold.

CHICKEN SOUR CREAM SALAD

Use 1 chicken breast instead of baby corns and beans. To boil chicken breast, put it with ½ cup water and ¼ tsp salt in a pressure cooker. Pressure cook to give 1 whistle and simmer on low heat for 3-4 minutes. Remove from fire. Remove meat from bones. Shred the chicken and add to the salad.

Celery...
Only the stalks are edible, use leaves as a garnish.

Indian Vegetarian Dishes

How to make a simple dish turn exotic...Tasty Tips

Add crushed seeds of 1-2 chhoti illaichi (green cardamoms) to a curry to make it differently delicious!

Add 1 crushed laung (clove) to a stir- fried or masala dish. Makes a world of difference!

KADHAI BABY CORNS

Picture on page 86

Corns in the usual kadhai masala, flavoured with fenugreek and coriander.

INGREDIENTS

Serves 4

200 gm baby corns
juice of ½ lemon
2 capsicums - cut into thin fingers
1-2 dry red chillies - deseeded
1½ tsp saboot dhania (coriander seeds)
a pinch of methi daana (fenugreek seeds)
1" piece ginger and 6- 8 flakes of garlic - crushed to a paste (2 tsp paste)
2 onions - chopped
4 tomatoes
1 tbsp kasoori methi (dry fenugreek leaves)
¼ tsp haldi, ½ tsp garam masala
½ tsp amchoor, 1¼ tsp salt, or to taste
2 tbsp chopped coriander
½" piece ginger - cut into match sticks or shredded on the grater (1 tsp)
5 tbsp oil

METHOD

1 Boil 4 cups water. Add whole tomatoes, 1 tsp salt, 1 tbsp lemon juice and babycorn. Boil them for 2-3 minutes. Remove from fire. Strain through a sieve (channi). Put babycorn under running water (refresh). Let them cool down. Cut into 2 pieces lengthwise, if thick or keep whole. Peel the tomatoes and chop finely.

2 Warm red chillies and dhania saboot on a tawa, till slightly crisp and dry, for about 30 seconds.

3 Roughly grind red chillies and saboot dhania to a rough powder in a small spice grinder.

4 Heat 2 tbsp oil in a pan and add the boiled baby corns. Bhuno for 4-5 minutes till they start turning brown. Keep them spaced out while bhunoing and let them not overlap each other. Add the capsicum strips and stir fry for 2 minutes. Remove from kadhai and keep aside.

5 Heat 3 tbsp oil in a kadhai. Remove from fire. Add a pinch of methi daana. Let it turn golden brown.

6 Return to fire. Add onion. Cook till onions turn golden brown. Add garlic-ginger paste. Mix well.

7 Add dhania-red chilli powder. Stir for 30 seconds.

8 Add peeled and chopped tomatoes and stir for about 4-5 minutes on low heat till dry.

9 Add salt, kasoori methi, haldi, garam masala and amchoor.

10 Add fresh coriander. Mix well till oil separates. Add ½ cup water. Let it boil.

11 Add capsicum and stir fry for 3-4 minutes. Remove from fire and keep aside till serving time.

12 At the time of serving, add baby corns and ginger matchsticks. Cook for 2-3 minutes. Serve.

TiP

When fresh baby corns are not available, buy a tin of baby corns. There is no need to boil the tinned ones. Just wash and use.

PANEER MAKHANI

Paneer in red gravy made in butter. Babycorns & broccoli blanched in hot water and sauteed in butter can also be added to this gravy instead of paneer. Even malai koftas can be added to this gravy.

INGREDIENTS

Serves 4

50 gm paneer - cut into 1" cubes
(500 gm) tomatoes - each cut into 4 pieces
tbsp desi ghee or butter, 2 tbsp oil
-5 flakes garlic and 1" piece ginger - ground to a paste (1½ tsp ginger-garlic paste)
tbsp kasoori methi (dry fenugreek leaves)
tsp tomato ketchup
½ tsp jeera (cumin seeds), 2 tsp dhania powder, ½ tsp garam masala
tsp salt, or to taste, ½ tsp red chilli powder, preferably degi mirch
½-1 cup milk, approx., ½ cup water
½ cup cream (optional), 3 tbsp cashewnuts (kaju)

METHOD

1 Soak kaju in ½ cup warm water for 10-15 minutes.

2 Drain kaju. Grind in a small mixer to a very smooth paste using about 2 tbsp water.

3 Boil tomatoes in ½ cup water. Cover and cook on low heat for 4-5 minutes till tomatoes turn soft. Remove from fire and cool. Grind the tomatoes along with the water to a smooth puree.

4 Heat 2 tbsp oil and 2 tbsp ghee or butter in a kadhai. Reduce heat. Add jeera. When it turns golden, add ginger-garlic paste.

5 When paste starts to change colour, add the above tomato puree. Cook till puree turns dry.

6 Add kasoori methi and tomato ketchup.

7 Add masalas - dhania powder, garam masala, salt and red chilli powder. Mix well for a few seconds. Cook till oil separates and the masala turns glossy.

8 Add cashew paste. Mix well for 2 minutes.

9 Add water. Boil. Simmer on low heat for 4-5 minutes. Remove from fire. Keep aside to cool for about 5 minutes.

10 Add enough milk to the cold masala to get a thick curry, mix gently.

11 Add the paneer cubes. Keep aside till serving time.

12 To serve heat on low flame, stirring continuously till just about to boil.

13 Add cream, keeping the heat very low and stirring gently. Remove from fire immediately and transfer to a serving dish. Swirl 1 tbsp cream over the hot paneer in the dish. Serve immediately.

TiP

Remember to add milk only after the masala is no longer hot, to prevent the milk from curdling. After adding milk, heat curry on low heat.

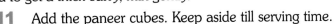

89

KHASTA BHINDI

Amazingly crisp and crunchy with a strong flavour of carom seeds.

INGREDIENTS

Serves 2-3

250 gm bhindi (lady fingers)
2 tbsp cornflour
1 tsp ajwain (carom seeds)
¼ tsp haldi (turmeric powder)
2 tsp chaat masala
½ tsp red chilli powder
1 tsp ginger or garlic paste
½ cup besan (gram flour)
½ tsp salt, or to taste
juice of ½ lemon (1 tbsp)
oil for frying

METHOD

1 Wash and pat dry the bhindi.

2 Cut the head and not the pointed end. Cut the bhindi into two pieces lengthwise.

3 Cut each piece further into 2 long pieces to get 4 pieces from each bhindi. Place in a shallow bowl or paraat.

4 Heat oil in a kadhai for frying.

5 Sprinkle cornflour, ajwain, haldi, chaat masala, red chilli powder, ginger or garlic paste, dry besan and salt on the bhindi in the paraat, mix well using both the hands.

6 Sprinkle lemon juice and mix well to coat the bhindi with the spices. Do not keep aside, fry immediately

7 Add half of the bhindi to hot oil and fry in 2 batches till crisp. Drain on paper napkins. Serve hot.

TiP *Mix all the ingredients to the bhindi at the time of frying as the salt added releases moisture which can make the bhindi soggy.*

KACHUMBER GOBHI

A dry minced preparation of cauliflower flavoured with fenugreek.

INGREDIENTS

Serves 4-6

- medium cauliflowers (phoolgobhi) - cut into small florets with a little stalk
- tbsp oil
- tsp jeera (cumin seeds)
- " piece ginger - chopped
- green chillies - deseeded and chopped finely
- ½ tsp haldi (turmeric powder)
- tsp red chilli powder
- tsp dhania (coriander) powder
- tsp garam masala
- tomatoes - chopped
- tsp salt, or to taste
- tbsp kasoori methi (dry fenugreek leaves)
- tbsp fresh coriander - chopped

METHOD

1 Wash and cut the cauliflower into small florets with 1" stalks.

2 Heat oil in a kadhai. Add jeera and let it turn golden.

3 Reduce heat. Add chopped ginger, chopped green chillies, haldi, red chilli powder, dhania powder and garam masala. Stir fry for a minute.

4 Add chopped tomatoes and cook for about 4-5 minutes, or till oil separates. The tomatoes will turn dry and glossy when oil separates.

5 Add the chopped cauliflower and 2 tbsp water and stir well. Add 1 tsp salt.

6 Cover and cook for 15-20 minutes or till the gobhi is done.

7 Add kasoori methi and stir well.

8 Serve hot sprinkled with fresh coriander.

Note: After getting cooked the gobhi becomes really kachumber. It almost gets the texture of minced gobhi.

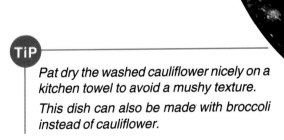

TiP

Pat dry the washed cauliflower nicely on a kitchen towel to avoid a mushy texture.

This dish can also be made with broccoli instead of cauliflower.

SHAHI MALAI KOFTA

Just follow the recipe step by step and see how simple it is to prepare this elaborate dish of koftas in a creamy whitish gravy.

INGREDIENTS

Serves 6

KOFTA
200 gm paneer (cottage cheese) - grated (2 cups)
1 boiled potato - grated
2 tbsp finely chopped coriander (hara dhania)
2½ tbsp maida (plain flour)
½ tsp each of garam masala and red chilli powder
¾ tsp salt, or to taste

TO COAT
2-3 tbsp maida (plain flour)

GRAVY
3 onions - ground to a paste in a mixer
4 tbsp kaju - soak in ½ cup hot water, 4 tbsp curd (dahi)
½ cup malai or cream or ½ cup milk
2 tbsp desi ghee or butter or 3 tbsp oil
1 tsp garam masala, ¾ tsp red chilli powder, ¼ tsp haldi
1 tbsp kasoori methi (dry fenugreek leaves), 1 tsp salt, or to taste
seeds of 3 chhoti illaichi (green cardamoms) - crushed

TiP

Whole mushroom sauted in butter, small potatoes boiled and deep fried, boiled corn and peas, Navrattan Curry (mixed vegetables, paneer and tinned pineapple) etc. can be used with this gravy.

METHOD

1. To prepare the koftas, mix grated paneer, potatoes, fresh coriander, red chilli powder, salt, garam masala and 2½ tbsp maida. Mix well till smooth. Make 12 balls.

2. Spread 2-3 tbsp maida on a plate. Roll each ball in maida. Dust to remove excess maida.

3. Heat oil in a kadhai for frying. Deep fry 1 kofta at a time in medium hot oil till light brown. Keep fried koftas aside.

4. Soak kaju in ½ cup hot water for 10 minutes. Drain away the water. Grind the softened cashews to a very fine paste with 4 tbsp curd in a small grinder. Keep cashew paste aside.

5. For the gravy, heat ghee in a heavy bottomed kadhai or a non stick pan. Add onion paste. Stir on low flame till it turns transparent and ghee separates and the sides of the kadhai look glossy because of the separated ghee. Do not let the onions turn brown by keeping on high flame. (Remember, we are making a white gravy and not a brown one!) Add haldi. Stir for a few seconds.

6. Add kaju-curd paste. Cook for 2-3 minutes on low flame. Add garam masala, red chilli powder and salt.

7. Add kasoori methi and stir for 2 minutes. Add 1 cup water to make a thick gravy. Boil on low heat for 3-4 minutes. Remove from fire and let it cool.

8. At the time of serving, add powdered chhoti illaichi and cream or milk to the gravy. Add enough milk to get the right consistency of the gravy. Keep on fire & bring to a boil on low heat. Add koftas and simmer on low heat for 1 minute. Serve garnished with a swirl of cream, roasted magaz and coriander leaves.

Caution!

If the paneer is kept in water, take the paneer out of the water an hour in advance. If wet paneer is grated, the koftas might break on frying.

Another caution!

Fry only one kofta at a time in hot oil on medium heat. Too many koftas at a time in oil, reduces the temperature of oil. End result...koftas break on frying.

CHATPATE BALTI ALOO

Serves 4

6 medium potatoes - peeled and cut into ¼" thick round slices
3 tbsp oil
½ tsp jeera (cumin seeds)
½ tsp saunf (fennel seeds)
½ tsp kalonji (nigella seeds)
½ tsp rai (mustard seeds)
¼ tsp methi dana (fenugreek seeds)
2 medium onions - sliced
½ tsp haldi (turmeric powder)
¾ tsp salt, or to taste
4 flakes garlic - chopped & crushed to a paste
½" piece ginger - chopped & crushed to a paste
2 dried, red chillies - crushed
a few curry leaves (2 tbsp)
1 tbsp green coriander - chopped
1 fresh red chilli (optional) - slit, remove seeds and slice into thin long pieces
1 green chilli - slit, remove seeds and slice into thin long pieces
1 tsp chaat masala

METHOD

1 Peel, wash and cut potatoes into ¼" thick round slices.

2 Heat oil in a kadhai or a non stick pan. Reduce heat slightly. Collect jeera, saunf, kalonji, rai & methi dana together and put in oil together. Fry for ½ minute till the saunf starts changing colour.

3 Add onions, bhuno until onions turn light golden. Add haldi. Stir.

4 Add garlic, ginger, red chillies and curry leaves, bhuno for 1 minute.

5 Add potatoes, salt and coriander. Mix well.

6 Add fresh red and green chillies, stir until well mixed.

7 Reduce to very low heat, spread out the potatoes in the kadhai. Cover tightly with a big lid, and cook for 10-12 minutes or until the potatoes are tender. Stir once or twice in between. Uncover and add chaat masala. Add more spices if required. Transfer to a serving platter and serve hot.

Crispy Vegetable

Keep the potatoes in a single layer while cooking. Do not overlap the pieces or they turn soft. Keep them spread out.

Variation:

Add 1 tbsp chopped cashewnuts and 1 tsp of kishmish for extra crunch at step 5.

TIL MIL MATAR ALOO

The most common vegetables - potatoes and peas with a twist. A dry dish.

INGREDIENTS

erves 4

potatoes
cup boiled or frozen peas (matar)
tbsp oil
½ tbsp safed til (sesame seeds)
tsp jeera (cumin seeds)
large onion - chopped very finely
-5 cashews (kaju) - split into two from the middle to get halves
0-15 raisins (kishmish) - soaked in little water
tsp salt, or to taste, ¼ tsp haldi (turmeric powder)
½ tsp garam masala, ½ tsp red chilli powder, ½ tsp amchoor
-3 green chillies - whole
.-3 tbsp chopped coriander
. tsp lemon juice

METHOD

1 Put potatoes in a deep pan (patila), cover them with water. Bring to a boil. Cook covered on low heat for 7-8 minutes till soft. They should feel soft when a knife is inserted. Do not over cook. (You may also pressure cook the potatoes to give one whistle. For a quicker subzi, microwave the potatoes if you wish — 4 potatoes would take about 4 minutes on full power).

2 Peel and cut each potato into 4 equal pieces.

3 Heat oil in a non stick pan or kadhai. Reduce heat. Add til and jeera. Wait till the til (sesame seeds) starts changing colour.

4 Add chopped onions. Stir until onions turn light brown.

5 Add kaju. Stir-fry for a minute. Strain kishmish from water and add to the onions. Stir.

6 Add salt, haldi, garam masala, red chilli powder and amchoor. Mix.

7 Add whole green chillies and fresh coriander. Cook for 1 minute.

8 Add 2-3 tbsp water. Mix.

9 Add the potatoes. Stir-fry gently for about 5-6 minutes on low heat, taking care not to break the potatoes. Keep the potatoes spread out in the kadhai/pan to get crisp potatoes.

10 Finally, add peas. Mix gently. Cook for 2 minutes stirring occasionally. Add lemon juice and mix well. Remove from fire. Serve hot.

> **TiP**
> *Store sesame seeds in the fridge. They acquire a foul taste and smell if kept for too long in a warm place.*

PAALAK PANEER

A quick and tasty way of making this evergreen spinach dish.

INGREDIENTS

Serves 4

½ kg paalak (spinach), choose a bundle with smaller leaves
3 tbsp oil
1 moti illaichi (brown cardamom)
2-3 laung (cloves), 3-4 saboot kali mirch (peppercorns)
3 onions - chopped
1" piece ginger - chopped
4-6 flakes garlic - chopped, 1 green chilli - chopped
1 tbsp kasoori methi (dried fenugreek leaves)
¾ tsp garam masala, ½ tsp red chilli powder
¼ tsp amchoor, 1¼ tsp salt, or to taste
2 tomatoes - chopped
100 gms paneer (cottage cheese) - cut into 1" cubes

BAGHAR (TEMPERING)
1 tbsp desi ghee or butter
1" piece ginger - cut into thin long pieces
1 green chilli - slit into long pieces
½ tsp red chilli powder

METHOD

1 Break paalak leaves into small pieces. Discard stalks. Wash in plenty of water. Keep aside to drain.

2 Heat oil in a kadhai. Add moti illaichi, laung and saboot kali mirch.

3 Add chopped onions and cook till light brown.

4 Add ginger, garlic and green chillies. Stir on low flame for 1 minute. Add kasoori methi.

5 Add garam masala, red chilli powder, amchoor and salt. Stir on low flame for 1 minute.

6 Add chopped tomatoes. Cook for 3-4 minutes, till well blended.

7 Add spinach and cook uncovered for 10-12 minutes on low flame. Remove from fire. Cool.

8 Blend the cooled mixture along with ½ cup water, just for a few seconds, to a coarse paste. Do not grind it too finely.

9 Boil 1 cup water and add the spinach paste to it. Simmer, covered for 4-5 minutes.

10 Cut paneer into 1" cubes, leaving aside some for garnishing. Deep fry to a golden colour.

11 Mix paneer pieces in the cooked spinach. Give it one boil. Simmer for 2-3 minutes till paneer turns soft. Transfer to a serving dish.

12 Heat 1 tbsp desi ghee or butter. Add ginger and green chilli. Remove from fire. Add red chilli powder and pour oil on the hot paalak. Mix lightly. Serve.

TiP

You can forget frying the paneer if you wish!

ARBI AJWAINI

Arbi combined with a masala of onion rings flavoured with carom seeds. A dry dish.

INGREDIENTS

erves 4

½ kg arbi (colocasia)
onions - peel and cut into circles & separate the rings
2" piece ginger - chopped finely
-3 green chillies - cut into thin long pieces and deseeded
¼ tsp haldi (turmeric powder)
tomatoes - chopped
tsp ajwain (carom seeds)
½ tsp jeera (cumin seeds)
tsp dhania (coriander) powder
½ tsp salt, or to taste
½ tsp red chilli powder
½ tsp amchoor (dried mango powder)
½ cup chopped coriander

METHOD

1 Cut onion into circles and separate into rings.

2 Pressure cook arbi with 3 cups water and 2 tsp salt to give one whistle. Keep on low flame for 4 minutes. Do not over boil. Remove from fire. After the arbi cools, peel and flatten thinly each piece between the palms.

3 Heat 2 cups oil in a kadhai for frying. Put 4-5 pieces of flattened arbi at one time in oil. Fry till golden brown. Remove from oil.

4 When cool, cut each piece diagonally into ½" thick slices. Keep aside.

5 Heat 2 tbsp oil in a clean kadhai. Reduce flame. Add ajwain and jeera. Cook till jeera turns golden.

6 Add onion rings and cook till light brown. Add haldi and mix for 30 seconds.

7 Add tomatoes and cook for 2 minutes till soft. Add ginger and stir for a minute.

8 Add chilli powder, amchoor, salt and dhania powder. Stir to mix well. Add 2-3 tbsp water. Boil.

9 Add fried arbi. Mix well.

10 Add hara dhania and green chillies. Stir fry for 2 minutes. Serve.

TiP

If the arbi is not boiled in salted water, add a little extra salt.

You can grill the arbi instead of frying. To grill, spread the boiled arbi on a plate. Sprinkle some salt, red chilli powder and 3-4 tbsp besan. Sprinkle 3 tbsp thick curd and mix well. Grill in an oven on a greased wire rack till brown specs appear.

MATAR PANEER CURRY

The most common dish of Punjab, but yet liked by everyone.

INGREDIENTS

Serves 4

200 gms paneer - cut into 1" cubes
1 cup shelled peas
2 onions
1" piece ginger
3 tomatoes
seeds of 1 moti illaichi (brown cardamoms)
2 cloves (laung)
¼ cup well beaten curd (beat till smooth with a wire whisk)
1 tsp dhania (coriander) powder
½ tsp red chilli powder, ¼ tsp amchoor
¼ tsp garam masala
4-5 tbsp oil

METHOD

1 Grind onions, ginger, laung, moti illaichi and tomatoes to a smooth puree in a mixer.

2 Heat oil in a kadhai. Add the onion - tomato puree. Cook covered on high flame for about 5 minutes till dry. Remove cover and cook, stirring frequently for 5-7 minutes till very thick and absolutely dry.

3 Add dhania powder, red chilli powder, amchoor and garam masala. Reduce heat and cook for 5 minutes more till oil separates. The masala should be dry and look glossy because the oil separates which makes the masala as well as the sides of the kadhai turn glossy.

4 Beat curd with a wire whisk or fork till very smooth.

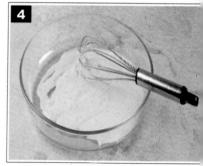

5 Add well beaten curd to the masala, stir continuously for about 3-4 minutes, till oil separates again and the masala turns to a bright red colour.

6 Add enough water, about 2½ cups water, to get a thick gravy. Add salt to taste, about 1 tsp salt. Cover and cook the gravy for about 5 minutes on low heat till oil separates and comes to the surface.

7 Add peas. Cook covered till peas are done.

8 Add paneer and ¼ tsp garam masala. Cook on low heat for 3-4 minutes till paneer gets soft. Serve hot.

Has the oil separated from the masala? Is it time to add water or should I stir fry the masala some more?

Sometimes when we do not add too much oil for home cooked meals, the oil actually does not separate and float on the surface. So, when the masala stops sticking to the bottom of the kadhai and starts to collect in the centre as a ball, it is done. The sides of the kadhai or the pan get glossy with oil too. Go ahead and add the water or any other liquid like milk or coconut milk, to get the gravy.

PUNJABI KADHI

Makes a perfect Sunday lunch with boiled rice. A little baking powder in the pakoras make them melt in the mouth!

Serves 4-6

½ cup besan (gram flour)
2 cups khatti dahi (sour yogurt)
½ tsp haldi powder, 2½ tsp salt or to taste, ¾ tsp red chilli powder (according to taste)

OTHER INGREDIENTS
4 tbsp oil
½ tsp jeera (cumin seeds), ½ tsp methi daana (fenugreek seeds)
2 moti illaichi (black cardamoms), 2 laung (cloves), 3-4 dry, red chillies

PAKORE (DUMPLINGS)
1 cup besan (gram flour), 1/3 cup water- approx.
1 big onion - chopped finely, 1 small potato - chopped finely
1" piece ginger - chopped finely, 2 green chillies - chopped finely
½ tsp red chilli powder, 1 tsp salt, ½ tsp garam masala, 1 tsp dhania powder
pinch of baking powder, oil for frying

TADKA/TEMPERING
2 tbsp oil, ½ tsp jeera (cumin seeds), ¼ tsp red chilli powder

METHOD

1. Mix khaati dahi, besan, salt, haldi, red chilli powder and 5 cups water. Beat well till smooth and no lumps remain.
2. In a big heavy-bottomed pan, heat oil. Add jeera, methi daana, moti illaichi and laung. Add whole, red chillies too.
3. When jeera turns golden, add curd-water mixture. Stir continuously till it boils. After one good boil, lower heat and simmer for 15-20 minutes, stirring occasionally. Remove from fire and keep aside. The kadhi thickens more on keeping.
4. To prepare pakoras, mix besan with water to make a thick paste. Beat well. Add all other ingredients given under pakoras. Beat well to get a soft dropping batter.
5. Heat oil and drop spoonfuls of batter. Deep fry 5-6 pakoras at a time, on medium heat till golden brown and crisp. Keep aside.
6. At serving time, add pakodas to kadhi and bring to a boil. Simmer for 1-2 minutes. Transfer the hot kadhi to a serving dish.
7. For tadka, heat oil in small pan. Reduce flame and add jeera. When it turns golden, remove from fire & add red chilli powder. Pour hot oil on the hot kadhi in the dish. Mix lightly. Serve hot with boiled rice.

Indian Non-Vegetarian
The right method of cooking chicken

For 1 kg of chicken with bones, stir fry (bhuno) the chicken for 8-10 minutes on medium heat till it turns brownish. Reduce heat and cook covered on low heat for another 8-10 minutes or till tender. To check, break a piece, if it pulls off easily it is done. Tomatoes or liquid in any form, should always be added to the chicken after stir frying it. Stir frying in the beginning seals in the juices of the chicken and the chicken is tastier after getting cooked.

MUTTON MASALA

Picture on page 102

Ensure that you buy good quality mutton otherwise it takes very long to make it tender.

INGREDIENTS

Serves 2-3

½ kg mutton with bones or ½ kg mutton chops
4 medium onions - chopped
5- 6 tbsp pure ghee or oil
1 tej patta (bay leaf)
8- 10 flakes of garlic- crushed to a paste (1 tbsp)
1" piece of ginger - crushed to a paste (1 tbsp)
¾ tsp salt
¾ tsp red chilli powder
¾ tsp garam masala
½ tsp haldi powder (turmeric powder)
1 tsp dhania powder (coriander powder)
¾ tsp jeera - powdered (cumin powdered)
4 large tomatoes- cut into pieces and puree in a mixer

GARNISHING
sliced green chillies and ginger strips

METHOD

1 In a pressure cooker heat oil or ghee. Add tej patta and chopped onion. Stir fry for 4- 5 minutes on medium flame till onions turn light brown.

2 Add ginger and garlic paste. Fry for 1 minute.

3 Add mutton and cook for 15 minutes on medium heat, stirring in between after every few minutes.

4 Add fresh tomato puree. Mix well. Stir for 10- 12 minutes on high flame.

5 Add salt, red chilli powder, garam masala, haldi, dhania and jeera powder. Mix well and cook for 3-4 minutes.

6 Add 1 cup water. Mix well and close the cooker.

7 Give 2 whistles. Keep on low heat for 15 minutes. Remove from fire. Let the pressure drop by itself.

8 Transfer to a serving dish, garnish with green chillies and ginger strips and serve with hot chappatis or paranthas.

TIP

The bhunoing of mutton at step 3 should be done patiently. All the water should dry up and the mutton should give a nice well fried look.

icture on page 103

RESHMI CHICKEN MASALA

The chicken pieces are coated with curd & besan and fried to make them as soft as silk.

INGREDIENTS

erves 4

0 gms boneless chicken - cut into 2" pieces (8-10 pieces)
 cup milk

PASTE
eeds of 3 chhoti illaichi (green cardamoms)
" stick dalchini (cinnamon), ¾ tsp saunf (fennel)
 saboot kali mirch (peppercorns), 2 laung (cloves)
 tsp jeera (cumin seeds), 2 tsp saboot dhania (coriander seeds)
" piece ginger, 2-3 flakes garlic
 tsp red chilli powder, ¾ tsp salt

COATING
 tbsp besan (gramflour), 6 tbsp curd
 tbsp chopped fresh dhania (coriander)
 tsp salt, ¼ tsp red chilli powder, ¼ tsp ajwain (carom seeds)

OTHER INGREDIENTS
 capsicums - cut into 1" pieces
 onions - cut into 4 pieces
 cup tomato puree (readymade), ½ tsp garam masala, ½ tsp salt or to taste

METHOD

1 Grind together all the ingredients of paste in a small spice grinder to a smooth paste with a little water if required. Keep the ground masala paste aside.

2 Cut onion into 4 pieces and capsicum into 1" pieces.

3 Mix together ¾ cup milk with ¼ cup water. Heat and bring to a boil.

4 Add the above ground masala to the milk.

5 Add chicken also to the milk. Give 1-2 boils. Cover and lower heat. Cook for 8-10 minutes or till chicken is tender. Increase heat and cook till completely dry. Remove from fire. Cool.

6 To the cooked chicken add all coating ingredients. Mix well.

7 Heat oil and fry few (2-3) pieces at a time on low heat till golden brown colour.

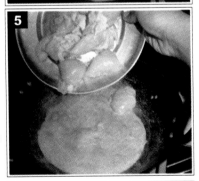

8 Heat 2 tbsp oil in a kadhai. Add tomato puree. Cook for 3-4 minutes till dry and oil separates.

9 Add onion and capsicum. Stir fry for 2 minutes. Add salt and ¼ cup water. Bring to a boil.

10 Add fried pieces of chicken. Sprinkle garam masala. Mix for 1 minute till the chicken turns hot and soft. Serve.

TiP

Mix fried chicken lightly with the tomato puree so that the coating doesn't come out.

KADHAI MURG

A semi- dry preparation of chicken, flavoured with fenugreek and coriander.

INGREDIENTS

Serves 4-6

1 medium sized (800 gms) chicken - cut into 12 pieces
6-7 tbsp oil
½ tsp methi dana (fenugreek seeds), 3 whole, dry red chillies
3 large onions - cut into slices
15-20 flakes garlic - crushed & chopped
1" pieces of ginger - crushed to a paste (1 tbsp)
4 large tomatoes - chopped
½ cup ready-made tomato puree
1 tbsp saboot dhania (coriander seeds)
1 tsp red chilli powder, 1 tsp dhania powder (ground coriander)
2 tsp salt, or to taste, ¼ tsp amchoor, ½ tsp garam masala
½ cup chopped green coriander
1 capsicum - cut into slices
1" piece ginger - cut into match sticks
1-2 green chillies - cut into long slices
½ cup cream, optional

METHOD

1 Put saboot dhania (coriander seeds) on a tawa. Keep on fire and roast lightly till it just starts to change colour. Do not make them brown. Remove from fire.

2 Crush the saboot dhania on a chakla-belan (rolling board and pin) to split the seeds. Keep aside.

3 Heat oil in a kadhai. Reduce heat. Add methi dana and whole red chillies and stir for a few seconds till methi dana turns golden.

4 Add onion and cook on medium heat till light brown.

5 Add garlic and stir for 1 minute. Add ginger paste.

6 Add the saboot dhania, red chilli powder and dhania powder.

7 Add chicken and bhuno for 8- 10 minutes on high flame, stirring well so that chicken attains a nice golden brown colour.

8 Add chopped tomatoes. Cook for 4-5 minutes.

9 Add salt, amchoor and garam masala. Cover and cook for 10-15 minutes till tender, stirring occasionally.

10 Add tomato puree and chopped green coriander. Cook for 2 minutes.

11 Add the capsicum, ginger match sticks and green chilli slices. Mix well.

12 Reduce heat. Add cream. Mix well for 2-3 minutes and remove from fire. Serve hot.

CHICKEN BHARTA

Serves 4

500 gms boneless chicken - very finely chopped
3 onions - chopped
1½ tbsp saboot dhania
2 dry red chillies - break into small pieces
1½" piece ginger- chopped
10 flakes garlic - chopped
3 tomatoes - chopped
1 big tomato - puree in a mixer
1½ tsp salt, 1 tsp garam masala, 1 tsp dhania powder
½ tsp amchoor
2 green chillies - keep whole, do not chop
2 tbsp chopped coriander
2 tbsp kasoori methi (dry fenugreek leaves)

1   Put saboot dhania (coriander seeds) and red chillies on a tawa. Keep on fire and roast lightly till it just starts to change colour. Do not make them brown. Remove from fire.

2   Crush the saboot dhania on a chakla-belan (rolling board and pin) to split the seeds. Break the red chillies with hands into small bits. Keep aside.

3   Cut boneless chicken into thin long strips and cut each of this strip into small pieces.

4   Heat 5 tbsp oil in a kadhai and add chopped onion, cook till golden brown.

5   Add crushed roasted saboot dhania, ginger and garlic. Stir for 30 seconds.

6   Add chicken and bhuno for 4-5 minutes on medium heat.

7   Add chopped and pureed tomatoes and dry red chillies, cook for 4-5 minutes.

8   Add salt, garam masala, dhania powder, amchoor. Mix well. Cover and cook on low heat for 6-8 minutes on low heat.

9   Lower heat, stir, add whole green chillies. Cook for 4-5 minutes or till done.

10 Garnish with fresh coriander and kasoori methi and serve hot.

BUTTER CHICKEN

An all time favourite!

INGREDIENTS

Serves 4

1 medium sized chicken (800 gm) - cut into 12 pieces

MARINADE
1 tbsp garlic paste or 8-10 flakes of garlic - crushed to a paste
1 tsp ginger paste or ½" piece of ginger - crushed to a paste
1 tbsp kasoori methi (dry fenugreek leaves)
few drops of orange red colour
½ tsp kala namak (black salt)
1 tsp garam masala

MAKHANI GRAVY
2 tbsp butter
2-3 tbsp oil
1 tej patta (bay leaf)
2 tbsp ginger-garlic paste or 2" piece of ginger and 16- 18 flakes of garlic- crushed to a paste
4 tbsp kaju (cashewnuts)
¼ tsp Kashmiri laal mirch or degi mirch
1 cup milk, 2 tbsp cream
½ tsp garam masala
1 tsp tandoori masala (optional)
¼ tsp sugar or to taste
½ kg (6-7) tomatoes - blanched, peeled and ground to a very smooth puree or 2 cups ready-made tomato puree
1 tsp salt, or to taste

METHOD

1. Soak kaju in hot water for 15 minutes, drain and grind to a very fine paste with a little water in a mixer.

2. Wash the chicken well. Pat dry chicken with a clean kitchen napkin.

3. For the marinade, mix garlic and ginger paste, kasoori methi, kala namak, garam masala and colour. Rub the chicken with this mixture. Keep aside for 15 minutes in the fridge.

4. Heat 6 tbsp oil in a kadhai, add marinated chicken, cook on high heat for 7- 8 minutes, stirring all the time. Reduce heat and cook covered for 10- 15 minutes or till tender. Add ½ tsp salt. Mix well. Remove from fire. Keep aside.

5. To prepare the makhani gravy, boil water in a pan. Add tomatoes to boiling water. Boil for 3-4 minutes. Remove from water and peel. Grind to a smooth puree. Keep aside.

6. Heat butter and oil together in a kadhai. Add tej patta. Stir for a few seconds. Add ginger and garlic paste, cook until liquid evaporates and the paste just changes colour.

7. Add pureed tomatoes or ready-made puree, degi mirch and sugar. Cook until the puree turns very dry and oil starts to float on top.

8. Add prepared kaju paste, stir for a few seconds on medium heat till fat separates. Lower the heat. Add about 1 cup of water to get the desired gravy. Bring to a boil, stirring constantly.

9 Add cooked chicken and salt. Cover and simmer for 5-7 minutes till the gravy turns to a bright colour. Reduce heat. Add milk on very low heat and bring to a boil, stirring continuously. Keep stirring for 1-2 minutes on low heat till you get the desired thickness of the gravy.

0 Remove from fire and stir in cream, stirring continuously. Add garam masala and tandoori masala. Stir. Garnish with 1 tbsp of fresh cream, slit green chillies and coriander. Serve hot with nan.

PUNJABI CHICKEN CURRY

INGREDIENTS

Serves 4-5

1 medium size chicken with bones (700-800 gm) - cut into 12 pieces
10 tbsp oil
1 tej patta (bay leaf)
4 laung (cloves)
1" stick dalchini (cinnamon)
4 moti illaichi (brown cardamoms)
4 tomatoes - puree in a mixer
1½ tsp salt, or to taste
½ tsp red chilli powder
2 tbsp dhania powder, ½ tsp haldi
1 tsp garam masala
2 tbsp chopped coriander (hara dhania)
½ cup thick curd - well beaten

PASTE
5 large onions
1½" piece of ginger and 10-12 flakes of garlic

METHOD

1 Heat oil in a heavy bottomed kadhai. Add 1 bay leaf, laung, dalchini and moti illaichi. Wait for a few seconds.

2 Add onion-ginger paste. Stir fry on medium heat till well browned.

3 Put the chicken pieces, bhuno nicely for 15-20 minutes on medium heat till the water evaporates and the chicken turns brown and glossy (The chicken leaves its own fat).

4 Add the freshly pureed tomatoes. Cook for about 8-10 minutes. Stir after every few minutes. Sprinkle a little water in between. Cook till oil separates and the tomatoes blen well with the onions.

5 Reduce heat. Add salt, red chilli powder, dhania powder, haldi and garam masala. Stir for 1 minute.

6 Reduce heat and add the curd. Bhuno for 6-8 minutes more, till the curd dries completely and o separates.

7 Add 2½ cups of water. Boil. Cover and cook on low heat for 3-4 minutes till the chicken turns tender c pressure cook to give 1 whistle. Remove from fire and serve hot garnihsed with coriander.

Seekh in Gravy

Serves 6

400 gms ready-made seekh kebabs - cut into ½"-¾" thick slices
5- 6 tbsp oil

ONION PASTE
2 onions - ground to a paste
15- 20 flakes of garlic, 3" piece ginger

KAJU PASTE (GRIND TOGETHER WITH SOME WATER)
4 tbsp cashewnuts (kaju), 4 tbsp badaam (almonds)
seeds of 2-3 chhoti illaichi, seeds of 2 moti illaichi, 2 laung
½ tsp kalonji
1¼ tsp salt, ½ tsp garam masala
1½ tsp chicken masala

OTHER INGREDIENTS
6 tbsp oil, 1 tej patta (bay leaf), ½ tsp jeera (cumin seeds)
2 tomatoes - chopped
2 cups ready-made tomato puree
1 tsp Kashmiri laal mirch or degi mirch (optional)
¼-½ tsp sugar
1 cup milk
½ cup thin cream (optional)

METHOD

1   Grind all ingredients of onion paste and kaju paste separately in a mixer.

2   To prepare gravy, heat 6 tbsp oil together in a non stick pan or a kadhai. Add jeera and tej patta. Stir for a few seconds. Add prepared onion paste, cook until onion paste turns golden brown.

3   Add chopped tomatoes and cook for 6 minutes or till oil separates.

4   Add ready-made puree, degi mirch and sugar. Cook until the puree turns little dry and oil separates.

5   Add kaju paste, stir for ½ minute on medium heat till oil separates.

6   Lower the heat. Add 1 cup of water, give one boil.

7   Reduce heat. Add milk on very low heat and bring to a boil, stirring continuously. Keep stirring for 1-2 minutes on low heat till you get the desired thickness of the gravy.

8   Remove from fire and stir in cream, stirring continuously. Stir. Keep gravy aside.

9   Heat 5- 6 tbsp oil in a pan for frying. Fry chicken seekh pieces till golden brown from all the sides. Cook covered for 3-4 minutes. Remove from pan on paper napkins.

10   At serving time, add the fried seekh pieces to the gravy. Add more milk if the gravy appears thick. Check salt. Give one boil and heat thoroughly, remove from fire. Serve.

TOMATO FISH

INGREDIENTS

Serves 3-4

500 gm boneless fish - cut into 2" pieces
3 medium onions - chopped finely (1½ cups)
1 green capsicum - chopped finely
3 tbsp oil
¾ cup ready-made tomato puree
1 tsp chilli sauce
1 tbsp vinegar
½ tsp sugar
¾ tsp salt, or to taste
2 tsp cornflour

METHOD

1 Heat oil in a pan. Add onions. Stir fry till transparent. Add capsicum. Saute for a few seconds. Add tomato puree, chilli sauce, salt, sugar and vinegar. Mix.

2 Add fish in a single layer over the masala, without overlapping. Cook uncovered for 6-7 minutes on low heat. (Overturn the pieces of fish after 3-4 minutes). Cook till fish is properly cooked.

3 Remove the fish pieces with a slotted spoon on to a serving dish.

4 To the gravy in the pan, add cornflour dissolved in ¾ cup of water. Give one boil. Simmer for 2-3 minutes. Pour over the fish. Serve tomato fish with rice.

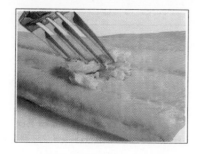

TiP

Checking fish for doneness - Place a fork in the thickest part of the fish, then gently twist the fork. The fish will flake easily when done.

To remove the fishy odour, rub a little lemon juice, salt and turmeric (haldi) on the fish and keep aside for at least 15-20 minutes. Wash and proceed.

ROGAN JOSH

The very popular Kashmiri mutton curry.

INGREDIENTS

Serves 2-3

500 gms mutton
7 tbsp ghee/oil
8 laung (cloves)
1" dalchini (cinnamon)
2 moti illaichi (black cardamom)
2 tej patta (bay leaf)
½ tsp hing (asafoetida) dissolved in 1 tsp water
1½ tsp saunf (fennel) - powdered
½ tsp sonth (dry ginger powder)
1 tsp ginger paste (½" piece of ginger - crushed to a paste)
4 onions - ground to a paste, 1 tsp ginger paste
¾ tsp red chilli powder (degi mirch)
1½ tsp salt, or to taste, ½ tsp pepper powder
7 chhoti illaichi (green cardamoms) - powdered
¼ cup curd (optional) - beat well till smooth
a little kesar (saffron) - dissolved in warm water

Options....

Some people do not like to add curd as the curd beats the colour. Then add 1 cup water and omit curd.

Some people add a little water in which ratanjot has been dissolved (to give a fiery red colour).

Amount of gravy is an individual choice. Some people keep little gravy where as others fry it to such an extent that only oil remains. Number of whistles will depend upon the quality of mutton.

METHOD

1 Heat ghee/oil in a cooker. Add laung, dalchini, moti illaichi and tej patta. Fry for 1- 2 minutes.

2 Add mutton and hing water. Fry for 15- 20 minutes till well fried. The mutton should become brownish in colour.

3 Add saunf, sonth, ginger paste, red chilli powder, salt and pepper. Fry for 3-4 minutes.

4 Reduce heat. Add powdered illaichi and curd. Keep stirring till it boils.

5 Add ½ cup water. Close the cooker and give 2 whistles. Keep on low heat for 10 minutes. (Mutton should become tender)

6 Open the cooker after the pressure drops. Add saffron. Simmer for 2-3 minutes and serve.

RAJMAH CURRY

INGREDIENTS

ervings 6

½ cups lal rajmah (red kidney beans) - soaked overnight in some water
½ tsp salt or to taste
 onions
-8 flakes garlic, 1" piece ginger
 tbsp oil
 tej patta (bay leaf)
 laung (cloves)
 moti illaichi (black cardamom)
 tomatoes - puree in a mixer
½ cup curd - beaten well till smooth
¼ tsp haldi, 3 tsp dhania powder, ¼ tsp amchoor
½ tsp garam masala, 1 tsp chilli powder, or to taste
 tbsp chopped coriander

METHOD

1 Pressure cook rajmah and salt together with about 10 cups water to give one whistle. Keep on low flame for 20 minutes. Remove from fire.

2 Grind onion, ginger and garlic to a paste in a mixer.

3 Heat 5 tbsp oil in a heavy bottomed kadhai. Add tej patta, moti illaichi and laung. Wait for 1 minute.

4 Add onion paste and stir fry till golden brown.

5 Reduce heat. Add haldi, dhania powder, amchoor, garam masala and red chilli powder. Stir for a few seconds.

6 Add tomatoes pureed in a blender. Cook till tomatoes turn dry and oil separates.

7 Reduce heat. Add beaten curd and stir continuously on low flame till the masala turns red again and oil separates.

8 Strain and add the rajmahs, keeping the water aside. Stir fry on medium flame for 2-3 minutes, mashing occasionally.

9 Add the water of the rajmahs and pressure cook to give 1 whistle. Keep on low flame after the first whistle, for 8-10 minutes.

10 Remove from fire. Add freshly chopped coriander leaves. Serve hot with chappatis or boiled rice.

I forgot to soak the rajmah at night? My husband/ boyfriend/ brother wants to eat rajmah-chawal this afternoon...

Use the famous quick soak method. Mix rajmah with tap water to cover and bring to a boil. Keep on low heat for 2 minutes, remove from fire and keep aside covered for 1 hour.

SAMBHAR

INGREDIENTS

Serves 4

1 cup *a*rhar ki dal (yellow lentil)
a small lemon sized ball of imli (tamarind)
5-6 flakes garlic - crushed to a paste (1 tsp)
½" piece ginger - crushed to a paste (1 tsp)
2 tbsp sambar powder
2 onions - cut into thin slices
½ tsp rai (mustard seeds)
½ tsp jeera (cumin seeds)
1 tbsp curry leaves
2 whole dried red chillies
salt to taste

METHOD

1   Clean, wash and pressure cook dal with 6 cups water and 1 tsp salt.
2   After the first whistle, keep on slow fire for 20 minutes.
3   Wash imli. Boil with 1 cup water. Cool. Extract the pulp. Keep aside.
4   Crush garlic and ginger roughly to a paste.
5   Heat 4 tbsp oil. Add rai, jeera and dried red chillies broken into bits. Wait till jeera turns golden.
6   Add the onions. Cook on low heat till onions turn dark brown. (Do not burn them).
7   Add curry leaves and sambhar powder. Cook for ½ minute.
8   Add imli extract. Boil for 1-2 minutes.
9   Add ginger-garlic paste. Cook for ½ minute.
10 Add the boiled dal. Add 1-2 cups more water if the sambhar appears thick. Add salt to taste. Boil for 5-6 minutes. Serve hot with idlis or rice.

DAL MAKHANI

erves 4-5

cup urad saboot (whole black beans) - soak atleast 2-3 hours,
r preferably overnight
tbsp desi ghee
½ tsp salt, 5 cups of water
cup ready made tomato puree
¼ tsp jaiphal powder (optional)
½ tsp garam masala
½ tbsp kasoori methi (dry fenugreek leaves)
-3 tbsp butter, preferably white

GRIND TO A PASTE
dry, whole red chillies, preferably Kashmiri red chillies - deseeded
& soaked for 10 minutes and then drained
" piece ginger, 6-8 flakes garlic

ADD LATER
½ cup milk mixed with ½ cup cream

1   Wash the dal and soak in warm water for atleast 2-3 hours or preferably overnight.

2   Drain water. Wash several times in fresh water, rubbing well, till the water no longer remains black.

3   Pressure cook dal with 5 cups water, 2 tbsp ghee, salt and ginger-garlic-chilli paste. After the first whistle, keep on low flame for 30 minutes. Remove from fire.

4   After the pressure drops, mash the hot dal a little with a kadchhi. Keep aside.

5   To the dal in the cooker, add tomato puree, kasoori methi, garam masala and jaiphal powder.

6   Add butter. Simmer on medium flame for 20 minutes, stirring dal occasionally. Remove from fire. Keep aside to cool till the time of serving.

7   At the time of serving, add milk mixed with cream to the dal. Keep dal on fire and bring to a boil on low heat, stirring constantly. Mix very well with a kadchhi. Simmer for 2 minutes more, to get the right colour and smoothness. Remove from fire. Serve.

Note: Originally the dal was cooked by leaving it overnight on the burning coal angithis. The longer the dal simmered, the better it tasted.

PINDI CHHOLE /MASALA CHANNA

INGREDIENTS

Serves 4

PRESSURE COOK TOGETHER
1 cup channa kabuli (Bengal gram)
¼ tsp soda- bi- carb (mitha soda)
2 moti illaichi (big cardamoms), 1" stick dalchini (cinnamon)
2 tsp tea leaves tied in a muslin cloth or 2 tea bags, 1 tsp salt

MASALA
2 onions - chopped finely
1½ tsp anar daana (pomegranate seeds) - powdered
4 big tomatoes - chopped finely
1" piece ginger - chopped finely
1 green chilli - chopped finely
1 tsp dhania powder, ½ tsp garam masala
½ tsp red chilli powder or to taste
2 tsp channa masala, 1¼ tsp salt or to taste

METHOD

1. Soak channas overnight or for 6-8 hours in a pressure cooker. Next morning, discard water. Wash channas with fresh water and add moti illaichi, dalchini, tea leaves, mitha soda, 1 tsp salt and just enough water to cover the channas nicely.

2. Pressure cook all the ingredients together to give one whistle. After the first whistle, keep on low flame for about 15 minutes. Keep aside.

3. Heat 4 tbsp oil. Add onions. Saute till transparent. Add anardaana powder. Cook stirring till onions turn brown. (Do not burn them).

4. Add chopped tomatoes, ginger and green chill. Stir fry for 5- 6 minutes.

5. Add dhania powder, garam masala and chilli powder. Mash and stir fry tomatoes occasionally for 8-10 minutes or till they turn brown in colour and oil separates.

6. Strain channas, reserving the liquid. Remove tea bag from the boiled channas.

7. Add the strained channas to the onion-tomato masala. Mix well. Stir fry gently for 5-7 minutes.

8. Add channa masala. Add the channa liquid. Check salt and add to taste. Cook for 15-20 minutes or medium heat till the liquid dries up and still a saucy consistency remains.

9. Serve garnished with onion rings, green chillies and tomato wedges.

CHANNE KI DAL WITH GHIYA

INGREDIENTS

Serves 4

1 cup channe ki dal (split gram)
2 small (200 gms) ghiya (bottle gourd) - peeled & chopped
½ tsp salt, ½ tsp haldi (turmeric powder), 2 tsp desi ghee or oil
½ tsp red chilli powder, tomato-onion baghar - given below

METHOD

1 Pick, clean and wash dal.

2 Mix dal, ghiya, salt, haldi, desi ghee, red chilli powder and 4 cups water in a pressure cooker.

3 Pressure cook for 5 minutes on low flame after the first whistle. Remove from fire.

4 Prepare tomato-onion baghar as given below and pour over the hot cooked dal. Mix gently. Serve hot.

BASIC TEMPERING OF DALS

Tadka/Chownk/Baghar

Dals taste good if they are tempered well. These two basic temperings can be poured over any dal.

Dehusked dals like dhuli moong, masoor and urad can be made by boiling each cup of dal with 3 cups water, 1 tsp salt and ½ tsp haldi in a deep pan till soft. Cover the dals, but not fully, leaving some space for the steam to escape otherwise the dal will boil over. Boil dal on high heat first and then reduce heat and cook till soft but not mushy. Whole dals cook better in a pressure cooker and each cup of whole (saboot) dal like masoor or moong needs about 4 cups water to get cooked with the right consistency.

TOMATO - ONION TADKA

INGREDIENTS

For 1 cup uncooked dal

3-4 tbsp ghee or oil, ½ tsp jeera (cumin seeds)
1 tsp chopped ginger, 1 onion - chopped finely, 2 tomatoes - chopped finely
1 green chilli - slit lengthwise into four pieces, ½ tsp garam masala (mixed spices)
½ tsp dhania (coriander) powder, 1/8 tsp amchoor (dried mango powder)
½ tsp red chilli powder

METHOD

1 Heat oil or ghee; reduce heat. Add jeera. When it turns golden, add ginger. Stir for 1 minute. Add onions.

2 Cook till onions turn brown. Do not undercook the onions. Brown them, stirring continuously.

3 Add tomatoes. Cook for 2-3 minutes on low flame.

4 Add dhania powder, amchoor and garam masala. Cook for ½ minute.

5 Remove from fire. Add the green chillies and red chilli powder. Mix well.

6 Pour over the hot dal. Mix gently.

HING - SARSON TADKA

INGREDIENTS

For 1 cup uncooked dal

3-4 tbsp oil, 1/8 tsp hing (asafoetida powder), ¼ tsp sarson (mustard seeds)
2 whole dry red chillies, a few curry leaves

METHOD

Hing

1 Heat oil; reduce heat. Add hing powder and wait till brown.

2 Add mustard seeds. Fry till they crackle, for about 1 minute.

3 Remove from fire. Add dry red chillies and curry leaves.

4 Mix well. Add to the hot cooked dal. Mix gently.

Continental

Continental food is served with a warm bread basket and some chilled butter. Bread may be in the form of bread rolls, bread sticks or simply bread slices. Sometimes a whole bread loaf may be cut into thick chunks of bread. Bread may be grilled till crisp or just be simply warmed in an oven. To serve, line a cane basket or any shallow dish or a tray with a cloth napkin. The napkin need not cover the sides of the basket completely. Serve bread on the container lined with the napkin. A small plate or bowl of butter with a butter knife should always accompany the bread basket. Sometimes rice too goes well with Continental food.

FOOL PROOF MEASUREMENTS FOR WHITE SAUCE ...ALL 2's

2 tbsp flour, 2 tbsp maida and 2 teacups milk

These measurements are for a normal white sauce. To make it thinner, add another ¼ cup extra milk and to make it thicker, make the milk less by ¼ cup.

A Good White Sauce

- Allow butter to cool slightly before adding flour to avoid lump formation.
- Do not allow the flour to brown as this reduces its thickening power.
- Cool roux (butter and flour mixture) slightly before adding liquid and add liquid gradually, stirring all the time.
- Boil sauce for a few minutes, otherwise sauce does not thicken properly, is raw in flavour, and lacks glossiness.
- If sauce is too thick—dilute with a little milk, bring to a boil again, and if too thin reduce by boiling rapidly with continuous stirring.
- To reheat a cold sauce, apply heat gently and stir or whisk vigorously.

CORN & CORIANDER BAKE

INGREDIENTS

Serves 4

1 cup tinned corn or niblets of 1 large corn (saboot bhutta), see note
1 small onion - chopped, ½ tsp crushed garlic, ½ tsp red chilli flakes
2½ cups milk
3 tbsp olive oil, 2½ tbsp cornflour, 1 tsp salt or to taste, ¼ tsp pepper
2 tbsp grated cheese (use tin or cubes)
3-4 tbsp chopped fresh coriander, preferably the stalks
½ tsp tabasco or capsico sauce (optional)

BASE LAYER
4 slices bread, 2 tbsp butter, ¼ tsp salt and ¼ tsp red chilli flakes
2 tbsp grated cheese (use tin or cubes)

GARNISH
tomato and capsicum rings

METHOD

1 For the base layer, break the bread slices into small pieces. Grind in a mixer to get fresh bread crumbs.

2 Melt 2 tbsp butter in a pan. Add the fresh bread crumbs, salt and red chilli flakes. Saute for 5 minutes or till bread turns crisp. Remove from fire.

3 Spread these buttered bread crumbs at the base of a greased oven proof dish. Sprinkle 2 tbsp grated cheese on the bread. Keep aside.

4 For the sauce, heat olive oil. Add onion and garlic, cook till onion turn golden brown.

5 Add cornflour. Cook on low heat for 1 minute.

6 Add the milk, stirring continuously. Add ½ tsp salt, ¼ tsp pepper and red chilli flakes. Stir till it comes to a boil.

7 When the sauce is thick, add the cheese and mix well.

8 Mix in the corn and coriander. Remove from fire. Add tabasco sauce.

9 Pour the mixture over the bread crumbs in the dish.

10 Decorate with capsicum and tomato rings.

11 Heat an oven at 200°C. Bake for 20 minutes or till golden.

Note: If using fresh corn, boil it in 3 cups water with a pinch of haldi, 1 tsp salt and 1 tbsp sugar added to the water, for about 5 minutes, to get sweet corn niblets.

TiP

Once grated, cheese quickly loses its bite. So it is best to grate only the amount you need for the recipe. Wrap the rest tightly in foil and it will keep for several months in the refrigerator.

PASTA IN TOMATO SAUCE

INGREDIENTS

erves 4

cups unboiled penne or any other shape pasta - boiled
medium capsicums - sliced into thin long fingers
medium tomatoes - sliced into thin long fingers
tbsp oil, 2 tsp crushed garlic
4 tsp pepper, 1 tsp oregano
cup ready-made tomato puree
½ tsp salt
½ cups milk

METHOD

1 To boil pasta, boil 8-10 cups of water in a large pan. Add 2 tsp salt and 1 tbsp oil. Add the pasta to the boiling water. Boil for 7-8 minutes or till the pasta turn soft but is still firm. Remove from fire and let the pasta be in hot water for 2-3 minutes. Strain. Refresh in cold water and strain again. Leave pasta in strainer for 15 minutes so that all the water drains out. Sprinkle 1-2 tbsp olive oil on the pasta and mix well. Keep aside.

2 Heat 1 tbsp oil in a kadhai, add ½ tsp garlic, wait for ½ minute. Add boiled pasta, saute for 1-2 minutes. Add ¼ tsp pepper and ½ tsp oregano. Mix, remove pasta from the kadhai.

3 In the same kadhai heat 3 tbsp oil. Add 1½ tsp crushed garlic. Wait till it changes colour.

4 Add 1 cup ready-made tomato puree. Cook for 3-4 minutes or till oil separates.

5 Add ½ tsp pepper, ½ tsp oregano and 1½ tsp salt. Mix. Reduce heat and cook for 2 minutes. Add boiled pasta, mix well. Keep aside.

6 At serving time, return the pasta on fire. Add capsicum, tomato and milk. Mix well. Check salt and pepper. Remove from fire. Serve hot with garlic bread.

TYPES OF PASTA

. Penne: (derived from the word *penna*, meaning pen). 3hort, hollow dried pasta, the thickness of a finger. Both nds are cut diagonally, suggesting the nib of a pen.

. Spaghetti: Long, thin, slightly thicker than noodles.

. Canneloni: Cylinder like, stuffed with a filling.

. Farfalle: Bow shaped or butterfly like pasta.

. Macaroni: small hollow shells, elbows, wheel or other shapes.

. Lasagne: (pronounced as *lazania*), long, broad sheets of pasta

. Fettuccine: (pronounced as *'fetuchini'*), long, flat ibbons of pasta, about ¼" broad. It is also called **agliatelle**. Different flavours like spinach, tomato, cheese etc. are available.

. Fusilli: Small spiral pasta.

TiP

Pasta is cooked to the "al dente" stage - tender but firm to bite. To test, press a piece against the side of the pan with a fork. It should need a firm pressure to break the pasta.

Use any other pasta shapes such as macaroni etc., if you have them at hand, instead of penne.

CHICKEN STROGANOFF

Cubed chicken simmered in tomato-cream sauce with mushrooms. A little yogurt is added along with the cream, to make the dish lighter.

INGREDIENTS

Serves 4

boneless chicken breasts (400 gm) - cut into ½" cubes
tbsp butter
small onion - finely chopped
00-150 gm mushrooms - each cut into two pieces
tbsp tomato puree, 1 tbsp tomato ketchup
tsp Worcestershire sauce
-4 flakes garlic - crushed & chopped
tbsp flour
cup cream
cup thick yogurt
tsp salt, ¼ tsp pepper and red chilli powder

GARNISH
capsicum - chopped

METHOD

1 Whip cream and yogurt well so that there are no lumps and is smooth. Keep aside.

2 Sprinkle some salt, pepper and chilli powder over the chicken pieces.

3 Heat 2 tbsp butter in a pan add onion and cook till light brown. Add the mushrooms and cook for 1 minute. Remove the mushrooms and onions from the pan.

4 To the same pan, add 1 tbsp butter, add chicken pieces and stir fry till golden brown. Cook covered for another 2- 3 minutes.

5 Add tomato puree, tomato sauce, worcestershire sauce, garlic, salt, pepper and chilli powder, mix well for 2 minutes.

6 Add flour, mix.

7 Reduce heat, take the pan off the heat. Add cream and dahi mixture, stirring with the other hand continuously. Mix well.

8 Return pan to heat, add chopped capsicum. Heat on very low flame gently for about 1 minute and remove just before it starts to boil. Serve with garlic bread or steamed rice.

TIP

Add chopped nuts, such as almonds or pine nuts, to the garnish for the extra crunch, if desired.

129

BAKED VEGETABLES

INGREDIENTS

Serves 8

WHITE SAUCE
4 tbsp butter
4 tbsp maida (plain flour)
3 cups milk
salt, pepper to taste
1 tbsp tomato ketchup

VEGETABLES
10-15 french beans - cut diagonally into pieces
2 carrots - cut into small cubes
½ small cauliflower - cut into small florets
½ cup shelled peas
1 medium potato - cut into small cubes
1½ cups chopped ghiya (bottle gourd) or 100 gm babycorns
cut into round slices

TOPPING
½ cup grated cheddar cheese (tin or cubes)
¼ cup bread crumbs
1 firm tomato - sliced

METHOD

1 To prepare the white sauce, heat butter in a clean heavy bottomed pan or kadhai, on low flame.

2 When butter melts, add the flour and mix stirring continuously on low flame for 1 minute. Do not let the colour change.

3 Remove from fire and add milk. Mix well. Return to fire and stir continuously till the sauce becomes thick and starts to coat the back of the spoon.

4 Add salt, pepper and tomato ketchup to it. Keep sauce aside.

5 Wash vegetables and pressure cook with 1 tsp salt with ¼ cup water, till the hissing sound starts. Remove from fire before the whistle. Cool.

6 Mix steamed vegetables along with the water to the prepared sauce. Keep on fire and bring to a bo stirring. Add salt if required.

7 Transfer to a shallow borosil dish. Arrange tomato slices over it. Sprinkle bread crumbs. Sprinkle cheese Bake in a hot oven at 200°C/400°F, till golden brown for about 20-25 minutes. Remove from the over and serve hot.

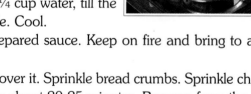

Mozzarella or Cheddar?

Mozzarella or pizza cheese is a melting cheese. This cheese on heating, melts and forms strings but unfortunately is less flavourful. Cheddar or processed cheese available in tins or cubes is very flavourful. It does not melt on cooking. To get the benefit of both cheeses, I like to mix half and half of both the cheeses.

For topping any baked dish or pizza use mozzarella as it melts and gives a nice look to the dish. To use inside any dish use cheddar as it is more flavourful.

TiP

If the top begins to brown too quickly, cover wit foil for last ten minutes of cooking time to preven the top from burning.

Ensure that all the vegetable pieces are cut i the same size in order that they all cook in th same time.

PASTA WITH MUSHROOMS IN CREAM SAUCE

Pasta with mushrooms in a white, creamy cheese sauce. The white sauce allows the mushrooms to retain their flavour unlike the acidic tomatoes.

INGREDIENTS

erves 4

cups uncooked fusilli pasta or any other pasta - boiled, see page 127 step 1
tsp oregano
00 gm mushrooms - sliced (1½ cups)
tbsp butter
flakes garlic - crushed, 2 tbsp maida (plain flour)
tbsp chopped parsley or coriander, 1½ cups milk
00 gm (1 cup grated) mozzarella or pizza cheese
½ cup fresh cream (100 gm)
alt to taste, a few black peppercorns (saboot kali mirch) - roughly powdered

GARNISH
-3 black olives - sliced, chopped parsley

Mushrooms

Store mushrooms in a loose paper bag or in a container which has air holes in it. They will sweat and get slimmy if they are kept too tightly wrapped.

METHOD

1 Melt 3 tbsp butter. Add sliced mushrooms and saute for 4-5 minutes.

2 Reduce heat. Add garlic. Stir for a few seconds.

3 Add flour. Cook on low heat for 1 minute.

4 Add parsley or coriander.

5 Remove from fire. Add milk, mix well to dissolve the flour. See that there are no lumps. Return to heat. Boil. Cook for 2 minutes, till it starts coating the spoon and turns a little thick. Remove from heat.

6 Add ½ cup cheese and cream. Add salt to taste. Keep sauce aside till the time of serving.

7 At the time of serving, heat 1 tbsp butter in a large non stick pan or kadhai and toss the pasta in it till it gets heated. Add oregano and ½ tsp salt, or to taste. Mix and remove from fire.

8 To serve, spread warm pasta on a plate. To heat sauce, keep on low heat and remove from fire when it is just about to boil. Pour hot sauce over the pasta. Sprinkle remaining cheese and crushed peppercorns. Serve garnished with black olives and parsley.

Chinese

How to boil noodles correctly to avoid them from turning mushy?

Overcooking of noodles is a major problem with beginners. To boil noodles the right way, boil 6-8 cups water with 1 tsp salt and 1 tbsp oil added to it. Add noodles to boiling water and boil them on high heat for about 1-2 minutes only. Never overcook noodles as they turn thick & mushy. They should be a little hard when you drain them. Do not make them soft.

Some noodles like glass noodles or fresh noodles available at the vegetable vendors do not need boiling. They are added to boiling water and the fire is shut off immediately. After being left in hot water for 2-3 minutes, they are strained when slightly soft.

Noodles are always rinsed in cold water to arrest the cooking process by stopping the heat. They have to be taken out of cold water several times till the water is no longer hot. If not done this way, they get slightly overcooked if they remain warm.

What is a seasoning cube and why is it added?

Vegetable stock is an important agent for most Chinese soups and sauces. However, if you do not have stock ready or feel lazy to make a stock, you can use seasoning cubes mixed in water instead to make a stock. Seasoning cubes are available as small packets. These are very salty, so taste the dish after adding the cube before you put more salt. Always crush the seasoning cube to a powder before using it. It blends well.

SPICY HONEY VEGGIES

Picture on page 133

Vegetables are coated with a sweet and spicy sauce. A delightful semi dry dish!

INGREDIENTS

Serves 4

1 large carrot
8-10 mushrooms - trim stalks and keep whole
8-9 baby corns - keep whole if small and divide into two lengthwise, if thick
1½ cups cauliflower or broccoli - cut into small, flat florets (¼ of a small flower)
1 onion - cut into 8 pieces and separated
1 capsicum - cut into ½" cubes
3 tbsp cornflour dissolved in ½ cup water with 1 seasoning cube
4 tbsp oil
2-3 dry, red chillies - broken into bits & deseeded, 15 flakes garlic - crushed
¾ tsp salt and ¼ tsp pepper, or to taste
a pinch ajinomoto (optional)
1½ tbsp vinegar, 1 tsp soya sauce
2½ tbsp tomato ketchup, 2-3 tsp red chilli sauce
3-4 tsp honey, according to taste

METHOD

1   Boil 4 cups water with 1 tsp salt. Peel carrot. Drop the whole carrot, mushroom, cauliflower and baby corns in boiling water. As soon as the boil returns, keep boiling for 1 minute. Remove from fire and strain the vegetables. Refresh veggies in cold water.

2   Cut parboiled (half cooked) carrot into ¼" thick round slices or flowers. To make flowers, make slits or grooves along the length of the boiled carrot, leaving a little space between the slits. Cut the grooved carrot widthwise into slices to get flowers. Cut capsicum into ½" pieces. Cut onion into fours and separate the slices.

3   Dissolve cornflour in ½ cup water. Add seasoning cube and keep aside.

4   Heat oil in a kadhai. Reduce heat. Add broken red chillies and garlic.

5   Stir and add onion, mushroom, baby corns, carrots and cauliflower. Add salt and pepper. Add ajinomoto. Stir for 1-2 minutes on high flame. Add capsicum. Reduce heat.

6   Stir and add chilli sauce, tomato sauce, soya sauce, honey and vinegar. Lower heat and stir for ½ minute.

7   Add the dissolved cornflour and seasoning cube. Cook till the vegetables are crisp-tender and the sauce coats the veggies.

How much soya sauce to add?

Soya sauce adds colour too besides enhancing flavour. Different types of soya sauce are available - dark & light. Also, if the soya sauce has been lying around in the house for a few months, it gets concentrated and even a small quantity of it, imparts a dark colour to the food. It is always better to add a lesser quantity of the sauce and add more later according to the colour of the dish. Too much soya sauce spoils the colour of the dish sometimes!

MONGOLIAN LOTUS STEM

Lotus stem in a sweet and sour Chinese sauce. A wet dish.

INGREDIENTS

Serves 4

200 gm lotus stem (Bhein)

THIN COATING BATTER

4 tbsp cornflour, 4 tbsp plain flour (maida)

½ tsp salt, ¼ tsp pepper

2 flakes garlic - crushed to a paste

¼ cup water, approx.

OTHER INGREDIENTS

1½ cups vegetables stock or 1½ cups water mixed with 2 vegetable seasoning cubes (maggi)

4 tbsp oil

3 spring onions - white part finely chopped and greens of onions cut into 1" pieces

10 flakes garlic - crushed

5 tbsp tomato ketchup, 1 tbsp vinegar

1 tsp salt or to taste, 1 tsp sugar

2 tbsp cornflour dissolved in ¼ cup water

METHOD

1 Peel lotus stem and cut diagonally into paper thin slices. To parboil (half cook) lotus stem, boil 4 cups water with 1 tsp salt. Add sliced lotus stem to boiling water. Boil for 2 minutes. Strain. Refresh in cold water. Strain, keep aside.

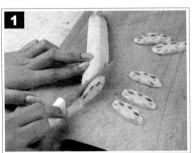

2 Mix all ingredients of the batter together, adding just enough water to get a thin coating batter.

3 Wipe dry the vegetable with a clean kitchen towel. Dip each piece in batter. Deep fry in two batches to a golden yellow colour. Do not brown them. Keep aside.

4 To make stock with cubes, mix 2 vegetable seasoning cubes with 1½ cups of water in a saucepan. Crush cubes. Give one quick boil and keep aside.

5 In a frying pan heat 4 tbsp oil. Add the finely chopped white part of green onions.

6 Add garlic. Remove from fire.

7 Add tomato ketchup, vinegar, salt and sugar. Return to fire and stir for ½ minute.

8 Add the prepared seasoning cube water or vegetable stock. Boil. Simmer for 2-3 minutes.

9 Add dissolved cornflour to stock, stirring continuously till the sauce just starts to thicken. Keep aside till serving time.

10 At serving time, add the lotus stem and green part of spring onions and cook for 1-2 minutes. Serve hot.

Variation: Try the recipe with paneer cut into 1" cubes, instead of lotus stem.

TiP

You can fry the lotus stem 3-4 days or even more in advance. When you take them out of oil after frying, spread them out on a tray in a single layer. Do not heap them. Let them turn cold. Store in a zip lock bag or box in the freezer compartment of the fridge.

CHICKEN IN HOT GARLIC SAUCE

INGREDIENTS

Serves 4

200 gms chicken breast (boneless)
1 tbsp finely chopped onion
1 tbsp chopped garlic
2 tsp red chilli paste or 1 tsp red chilli powder
3 tbsp tomato ketchup
¾ tsp salt, or to taste, ½ tsp sugar or to taste
¼ tsp aji-no-moto (optional)
2 cups chicken stock or water
2 tbsp cornflour
4 tbsp oil
1 tbsp vinegar, 2 tsp soya sauce, 1 tsp red chilli sauce
1 tbsp capsicum - cut into tiny cubes (diced)
2 tsp spring onion greens - finely chopped

MARINADE
1 egg, ¾ tsp salt
½ tsp aji-no-motto (optional)
1 tbsp cornflour, 1 tbsp oil

METHOD

1 Cut the chicken breast into even sized slices.
2 Marinate the chicken in all the ingredients of the marinade. Cover and keep in the refrigerator for atleast 2-3 hours.
3 Heat 4 tbsp oil in a wok and stir-fry the chicken for 3-4 minutes on medium heat. Drain and keep aside.
4 To the oil remaining in the wok, add onion, cook till soft.
5 Reduce heat. Add garlic & chilli paste. When garlic changes colour, add tomato ketchup, vinegar, soya sauce and red chilli sauce.
6 Add the capsicum and stir-fry for 1 minute.
7 Add chicken and cook for 1 minute. Stir-fry and add salt, aji-no-moto, sugar and stock or water. Boil. Cook on low heat till chicken turns tender.
8 Dissolve cornflour in 4 tbsp of water and add to the chicken, stirring continuously till it just starts to thickens. Add greens of spring onions. Remove from fire.
9 Serve hot along with boiled rice or noodles.

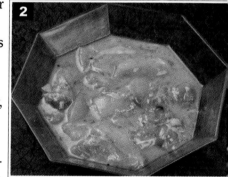

VEGETABLE FRIED RICE

INGREDIENTS

Serves 4

1½ cups uncooked rice (sela or parboiled rice), 2 tbsp oil
2 green chillies - chopped finely
2 green spring onions - chopped (keep green separate)
2 flakes garlic crushed & chopped - optional
¼ cup very finely sliced french beans, 1 carrot - finely diced
½ big capsicum - diced (cut into tiny pieces)
½ tsp salt, ½ tsp pepper, ½ tsp ajinomoto (optional)
½-1 tbsp soya sauce (according to the colour desired)
1 tsp vinegar - optional

METHOD

1 Wash rice. Boil 8-10 cups water in a big deep pan with 2 tsp salt. Add rice. Boil till almost done. Do not over cook. Strain. Leave in the strainer for 10 minutes. Spread the rice on a tray for 15-20 minutes.

2 Heat oil. Add green chillies. Wait for a few seconds. Add garlic and white portion of spring onions. Stir fry till onion turns soft.

3 Add beans, then carrots. Stir fry for 1 minute. Add capsicum.

4 Add salt, pepper and ajinomoto.

5 Add rice.

6 Add soya sauce and vinegar. Add the green portion of spring onion and salt to taste. Stir fry the rice for 2 minutes. Serve hot.

CHICKEN FRIED RICE

INGREDIENTS

Serves 4

1 chicken breast - cut into very small pieces
1½ cups uncooked rice (use sela or parboiled rice)
3 tbsp oil
1 onion - finely chopped, 2 green chillies - chopped
½ tsp ajinomoto (optional)
¼ of a cabbage - thinly sliced and chopped finely
1 carrot - finely chopped
½ tsp pepper powder, 1 tsp salt, ½ tsp sugar
2-3 tsp soya sauce
2 spring onions - diced upto the green portion

TiP

Sela rice (parboiled rice) is preferred to basmati rice for Chinese cooking. This is a hard grained, yellowish rice which does not stick at all after cooking.

METHOD

1 Wash rice. Boil 8-10 cups water in a big deep pan with 2 tsp salt. Add rice. Boil till almost done. Do not over cook. Strain. Leave in the strainer for 10 minutes. Spread the rice on a tray.

2 Heat oil in a wok or kadhai and fry onions till very light brown. Add chicken pieces and stir fry for 3- 4 minutes.

3 Reduce heat and cook covered for 5- 6 minutes or till chicken gets tender.

4 Add green chillies and ajinomoto. Add cabbage and carrot and stir fry for 1-2 minutes.

5 Add salt and sugar. Mix.

6 Add 2-3 tsp soya sauce. Mix well. Add rice. Mix well. Add pepper powder.

7 Add spring onions. Mix well, stir fry for a few seconds and remove from fire. Serve hot.

HAKA NOODLES

INGREDIENTS

Serves 4

CHILLI NOODLES
400 gms fresh noodles - boiled & spread in a tray (page 133)
4 tbsp oil
4-5 dry, whole red chillies - broken into bits, ½ tsp chilli flakes or powder
2 tsp salt, ½-1 tsp soya sauce

VEGETABLES
1 capsicum - shredded finely, 1 carrot - cut into fine juliennes or match sticks
1 cup shredded cabbage
6-8 flakes garlic - crushed and chopped - optional
2 spring onions or 1 small onion - shredded
2 tbsp bean sprouts - optional
1-2 tbsp dried mushrooms (soaked for 1 hour in water & washed thoroughly)
or finely sliced fresh mushrooms
1 tsp salt & ½ tsp pepper, ½ tsp ajinomoto (optional), 1 tbsp vinegar

METHOD

1 Heat 4-5 tbsp oil. Remove from fire, add broken red chillies and red chilli flakes or powder.

2 Return to fire and mix in the boiled noodles. Add salt and a little soya sauce. Do not add too much soya sauce. Fry for 2-3 minutes, till the noodles turn a pale brown. Keep the fried noodles aside.

3 To prepare the vegetables, shred all vegetables.

4 Heat 2 tbsp oil in a pan.

5 Reduce heat and add garlic. Cook for ½ minute.

6 Add vegetables in sequence of their tenderness - onions, sprouts, mushrooms, carrot and cabbage. Stir fry for 2 minutes. Add vinegar. Add capsicum.

7 Add ajinomoto, salt and pepper. Cook for ½ minute. Slide in the noodles and mix well.

CHAPATI OR PHULKA

INGREDIENTS

Serves 4

cups atta (whole wheat flour), ½ cup water - approx., 2 tsp ghee - optional

METHOD

1. Sift atta into a flat basin (parat). Add water gradually, and keep collecting the atta together till it can bind together. Form a ball of the dough. Now punch it down with your knuckles or hands to knead it to a smooth and soft dough. Knead for about 2-3 minutes to make it smooth. Wrap the dough in a thick damp cloth and keep aside in the same basin for atleast 30 minutes.
2. Knead the dough again for 2-3 minutes, when you start making the chapatis.
3. To make chapatis, make balls, slightly smaller than the size of a lemon.
4. Heat the tawa (griddle) on fire.
5. Roll balls into fairly thin rounds, about 5-6" in diameter.
6. Place the chapati on the hot griddle and reduce the flame. Cook the chapati on moderate heat throughout.
7. Turn over when tiny bubbles appear on the surface. Cook till brown spots are formed on the under surface.
8. Turn over and press lightly on the sides with a folded cloth till the chapati is puffed or bloated. Many find it more comfortable to remove the chapati from tawa and puff up the roti on direct flame with the help of tongs. But such rotis do not keep well. They are good if served immediately.
9. Apply ghee on one side if you like. Serve immediately or keep them wrapped in a clean cloth in an air tight box.

STEAMED RICE

All the water is absorbed by the rice in steamed rice.

INGREDIENTS

Serves 2

1 cup basmati rice, 2 cups water, ¼ tsp salt, 1 tsp lemon juice

METHOD

1. Wash rice in several changes of water till the water looks clean. Drain all water.
2. Put rice in heavy bottomed deep pan. Drain any water. Add 2 cups fresh water and keep aside for 20-30 minutes.
3. Keep the pan of rice on fire. Bring to a boil. Reduce heat and cover the rice with a tight fitting lid.
4. Keep on low heat for about 10-12 minutes or till the rice turns soft and absorbs all the water. Remove from fire. Fluff with a fork to let the steam escape so that the rice does not turn sticky.

BOILED RICE

Extra water is added for boiled rice which is later discarded when the rice is ready.

INGREDIENTS

Serves 2

1 cup basmati rice, 8 cups water, 1 tsp salt

METHOD

1. Wash rice in several changes of water till the water looks clean. Drain all water.
2. Keep a pan half full of water (about 8 cups) on fire. When the water boils, add the washed rice. Stir with a fork. Boil on medium heat for 6-7 minutes. Check a grain of rice to see if it is done. Remove from fire.
3. Strain and discard the extra water. Fluff with a fork to let the steam escape so that the rice does not turn sticky. Keep covered till serving time.

CHICKEN BIRYANI

The Hyderabadi style of layering rice and cooked chicken.

INGREDIENTS

Serves 6-8

2 cups uncooked long grain basmati rice - washed and strained
2 tsp salt, 1 tbsp oil, 3 tbsp ghee
seeds of 3-4 chhoti illaichi (green cardamoms) - crushed

FOR THE CHICKEN
1 chicken (700-800 gm) - cut into 12 pieces
4 large onions - chopped, 1½ tbsp ginger-garlic paste
2 large tomatoes - chopped
1 cup thick curd, 1 tsp chilli powder, salt to taste, 5-6 tbsp oil

GARNISHING
2 onions - sliced and deep fried in 1 cup oil till crisp and brown
½ cup poodina leaves (whole)
a few drops of orange colour or a few strands kesar (saffron)
dissolved in 1 tsp warm milk
2-3 drops of kewra essence (do not add extra)

METHOD

1 To cook the rice, boil 6-7 cups of water with 2 tsp salt and 1 tbsp oil. Add the rice to boiling water. Cook for just 4-5 minutes till almost tender. Strain and let it be in the strainer for 15 minutes so that all the water gets drained off. Run a fork through the rice to let the steam escape. With the help of a fork, spread the rice on a wide tray. Keep aside.

2 To cook the chicken, heat oil in a heavy bottomed kadhai. Add chopped onions. Stir fry till onions turn brown. Add 1½ tbsp ginger-garlic paste. Stir for ½ minute. Add chicken and bhuno for 15 minutes. Add chopped tomatoes. Cook till tomatoes turn absolutely dry. Add curd. Stir for a minute. Add salt, chilli powder and chicken. Bhuno for 2 minutes till the masala leaves oil. Add 1 cup water and cook covered till chicken turns tender. If there is any extra curry, dry it on fire. Keep on fire till you get a thick masala gravy. Remove from fire. Keep aside.

3 For assembling the biryani, take a large heavy bottomed metal handi or an oven proof glass dish, sprinkle some curry of the chicken at the bottom. Spread 1/3 of the rice. Place ½ the chicken pieces on it and wet the rice with 2 tbsp of masala gravy of the chicken. Sprinkle 1/3 of the fried onion and poodina leaves on it.

4 Repeat by adding rice, then chicken, sprinkle 2-3 tbsp curry, followed by poodina, fried onions. Finish with a top layer of rice sprinkled with some fried onions, and poodina.

5 Sprinkle chhoti illaichi powder, 2-3 drops of kewra essence and colour on the final layer.

6 Melt 3 tbsp ghee in a pan and pour on the biryani.

7 Cover pan with a tight fitting lid or aluminium foil. Place tawa on very low heat to reduce the heat further. Place the handi of rice on the tawa. If using a glass dish, keep in the oven at very low temperature, about 150°C. Keep for about ½ hour before serving for the flavourings to penetrate the rice.

Wash rice several times before cooking, changing the water, till the water looks clean.

SAADA PARANTHA

INGREDIENTS

Makes 6-7

½ cups atta (whole wheat flour)
cup water (approx.)
2 tsp salt, ½ tsp red chilli powder, ½ tsp ajwain (carom seeds)
2-3 tbsp ghee

METHOD

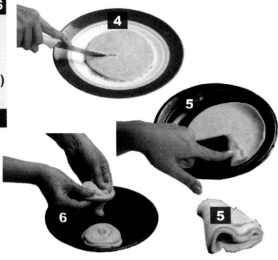

1   Mix atta, salt , red chilli powder and ajwain in a shallow bowl (paraat). Add water gradually, and keep collecting the atta together till it can bind together. Form a ball of the dough. Now punch it down with your knuckles or hands to knead it to a smooth and soft dough. Knead for about 2-3 minutes to make it smooth. Wrap the dough in a thick cloth and keep aside in the same bowl for atleast 30 minutes.

2   Divide the dough into 6 equal balls. Flatten each ball, roll out each into a round of 5" diameter.

3   Spread 1 tsp of ghee. Sprinkle a teaspoon of dry flour on the ghee.

4   Make a slit, starting from centre to the end.

5   Start rolling from the slit, to form an even cone.

6   Keep the cone upright. Press a little from the middle to flatten slightly.

7   Roll out, to a diameter of 5", applying pressure only at the centre and not on the sides.

8   Place a tawa on fire on medium heat. Put the parantha on the hot tawa. Turn side after a minute. Put ghee around the edges and spread some on top. Turn again and fry till golden. Remove on a cloth napkin and crush the parantha lightly along with the cloth so that the layers open up slightly.

Cracked and Hard Roti...

If you make roti from a freshly kneaded dough, they are bound to be hard. Always remember to make dough and keep it covered for atleast 30 minutes for gluten formation which makes rotis soft.

BHATURE

INGREDIENTS

Makes 8

2 cups maida (plain flour)
1 cup suji (semolina)
½ tsp salt, ½ tsp sugar, ½ tsp soda-bi-carb
½ cup sour curd, oil for deep frying

METHOD

1   Soak suji in ¾ cup warm water, which is just enough to cover it. Keep aside for 10 minutes.

2   Sift salt, soda and maida in a paraat or a shallow bowl.

3   Add sugar, soaked suji and curd. Mix very well. Add warm water little by little, mixing well till the dough collects in the centre. Knead well to make a firm dough. Do not make it too soft as on keeping it turns loose.

4   Knead again with greased hands till the dough is smooth. Pat some oil on the dough to prevent it from drying. Grease a polythene with oil from inside and put the dough in it. Tie a knot loosely. Keep it in a warm place for 3-4 hours or till serving time.

5   Make 8-10 balls. Roll each ball to an oblong shape. Pull from one side to get a pointed tip.

6   Deep fry in hot oil. Drain on paper napkins. Serve with channas.

MIXED VEGETABLE PULLAO

INGREDIENTS

Serves 4

1 cup uncooked rice - washed and strained and kept in the strainer for 30 minutes
3 tbsp oil
1 tsp jeera (cumin seeds)
2-3 laung (clove), 2 moti illaichi (black cardamom)
1 small stick dalchini (cinnamon), 1 tej patta (bay leaf)
2 onions - thinly sliced
1½ tsp salt or to taste, ¼ tsp haldi
½ cup shelled peas
1 small carrot - cut into small pieces
6-8 french beans - cut into small pieces

METHOD

1 Heat oil in a heavy bottomed pan. Reduce flame. Add jeera, dalchini, tej patta, laung and moti illaichi Stir fry till jeera turns golden.

2 Add onions. Stir fry till they turn transparent.

3 Add the vegetables and salt. Stir fry for 3-4 minutes.

4 Add rice and haldi. Mix gently. Add 2 cups of water. Boil.

5 Cover and cook on very low heat for 12-15 minutes, until the water is absorbed and the rice is done.

Variation

Mushroom Pullao - slice 100 gm mushrooms and use instead of the vegetables. Stir fry only the onions until light brown. Omit haldi also.

Jeera Pullao - Omit all vegetables and stir fry only the onions until brown. Omit haldi.

TiP

Do not hurry the process of cooking the rice, as it must absorb the liquid slowly in order for it to reach the correct softness when the liquid gets over. So cook rice on very low heat.

Soaking Rice...

Never soak rice. Always wash and strain. Leave them in the strainer for 30 minutes. Soaking makes the rice extra soft and sometimes the grains break while stirring them in oil.

Cakes & Cookies

To check if the cake is done, follow this sequence:

1. Touch the top gently, it should spring back and not form a depression.
2. See that the cake has shrunk away from the sides or in simpler words, has left the sides.
3. After you have seen the sides and touched the cake and it looks done, then only insert a knife in the highest part of the cake. If the knife comes out clean, the cake is done, if not then bake for 5-10 minutes more. When done, remove from oven after 10 minutes on to a wire rack.

What went Wrong with my Cake?

Quality of Cake	Reasons - any one or more of the following:
Heavy Cake:	Too little baking powder. Too much flour. Mixture (butter and sugar) not creamed enough. Flour mixed in too vigorously. Oven too slow (the cake takes too long to get done).
A Dry Cake:	Too much baking powder or flour. Not enough fat or liquid. Too long in the oven and gets overbaked and hard.
Sunken/Collapsed Cake:	Too much liquid. Too much baking powder or sugar. Too little flour. Oven door slammed or cake moved during baking. Taken out from the oven too soon.
Collapsed Cake with Heavy Streak at the Bottom:	Too much liquid used in mixing
Collapsed Cake with Thick Greasy Crust:	Too much fat
A Peaked Cake:	Insufficient butter/oil or baking powder/soda. Too much flour. Oven temperature too high.
A Badly Cracked Top:	Oven too hot. Cake tin too small. Too much flour. Not enough liquid.
Fruit Sunk to the Bottom	Fruit not properly dried and then coated with flour. Cake mixture too thin. Fruit added before adding the flour.
Close Texture:	Curdled mixture. If mixture curdles, beat mixture over hot water.
Open Texture and Dry:	Too much baking powder

Baking powder lying in the cupboard since many days...

Keep replacing baking powder and baking soda (mitha soda) after every 5-6 months. Before buying baking powder, check the manufacture date. Baking powder stays good for a year only. To check if it is effective, put ½ tsp in a cup of water. If bubbles form, it is usable, if no bubbles, discard!

143

Chocolate Cake

Extremely simple to prepare. Tastes good plain or with icing and even makes a perfect base for any dessert. Good for people who prefer to use oil instead of butter.

Makes 8-10 slices

4 large eggs
½ cup cocoa powder, 1¼ cups powdered sugar
¾ cup oil, 1 cup maida (flour)
1¾ tsp baking powder, ¼ tsp soda-bi-carb (mitha soda)
1 tsp vanilla essence

Always place the cake tin on a wire rack of the oven. It bakes much better.

METHOD

1 Beat eggs and powdered sugar with an electric egg beater till 4 times in volume and very frothy. If you do not possess an electric beater, beat the eggs and sugar in a pan kept on a smaller pan filled with boiling hot water (double boiler). The eggs are beaten over steam, taking care that the hot water does not touch the pan of eggs.

2 Add oil gradually to the frothy egg mixture and keep beating slowly. Add essence. Mix.

3 Sift maida, baking powder, cocoa & soda-bi-carb. Add ½ of the maida mixture to the egg mixture. Using a wooden spoon, with an upward and downward motion, fold in maida gently. Add the remaining maida. Do not over mix. Fold gently.

4 Transfer to a greased round tin of 8" diameter & bake at 180°C/350°F for 30-35 minutes.

5 Test the cake by inserting a clean knife in the centre of the cake. If the knife comes out clean, the cake is ready. Remove from the oven. Remove cake from the tin after 5 minutes.

Vanilla Cake with Oil

Use ½ cup cornflour instead of cocoa. Follow the rest of the recipe as it is.

Chocolate Butter Icing

Ice the chocolate or vanilla cake given above with this chocolate butter icing. Let the cake cool down completely and then cut into 2-3 layers depending on the height of the cake. In the picture, the icing is done only between 2 layers. If you like you can ice the top of the cake too as this icing is enough for inside and the top. If you like to only put the icing inside the cake, make half the quantity of icing. The top of the cake needs to be cut a little if it is not level. Always make the bottom of the cake as the top of the iced cake as it is very levelled.

1 cup (150 gm) white unsalted butter (not home made) - softened
2 cups icing/confectioner's sugar - sifted, 1 tsp vanilla essence, ½ cup cocoa powder

Never warm the butter to soften it. Just keep it outside the fridge for some time.

METHOD

1 Sift icing sugar and measure to 2 cups. Add cocoa to sifted sugar. Sift them together again. Keep aside.

2 Beat butter with an electric hand mixer till light, smooth and fluffy.

3 Add essence and sugar and cocoa mixture to the butter and beat to mix well to get a thick dropping consistency. If the mixture is a little thin which may be in summers, add 1 tbsp cornflour and if the mixture is too thick, add a few tbsp hot water to get a good spreading consistency, as in winters. If you like a darker colour, add more cocoa.

4 Cut the cake into 2 equal pieces. Spread 3-4 tbsp icing on cut side of each piece. Place one piece on a serving platter with the cut side up. Press the second piece of cake on it nicely to stick.

5 Top the cake with the remaining icing. Refrigerate for 30 minutes if the weather is warm. Dip a big knife in hot water and level the top icing with it.

6 Arrange some chocolate coated wafers and a sprig of mint leaves on the cake. Sift some powdered sugar on the cake through a strainer. If you wish, you can draw lines with a fork on top and sides of the cake. You can also arrange cherries, nutties or grated chocolate on it. Keep the iced cake in the fridge.

VANILLA BUTTER CAKE

This is the first cake I baked. An average egg weighs about 50 gms. All other ingredients used like maida, butter and sugar are equal in weight to the weight of the eggs in the recipe.

INGREDIENTS

erves 8

large eggs (200 gm), 1½ cups powdered sugar (200 gm) and 1/3 cups butter (200 gm), 2 cups maida (200 gm) tsp baking powder, 1½ tsp vanilla essence

METHOD

Creaming butter and sugar for butter cakes ...

To beat butter with sugar, the butter should be soft. Never warm the butter to soften it. Just keep it outside the fridge for some time till it becomes slightly soft.

1 Set oven for preheating at 180°C for 10 minutes.

2 Beat eggs in a clean dry bowl with a clean dry electric hand mixer and keep aside.

3 Beat butter and powdered sugar in a big deep pan with an electric hand beater till smooth and fluffy. Add essence and mix well.

4 Sift maida with baking powder. Keep aside.

5 Add half of the eggs and half of the maida mixture to the butter-sugar mixture. Beat well. Add the remaining maida mix and eggs. Beat for 3-4 minutes till the mixture appears light and fluffy.

6 Transfer to a greased square or round tin of 8" diameter and bake at 180°C/350°F for 35 minutes in the preheated oven on the wire rack.

7 Test the cake by (see page 143) inserting a clean knife or a tooth pick in the centre of the cake. If the knife comes out clean, the cake is ready. Remove from the oven. Remove cake from the tin after 5 min.

STIFF CHOCOLATE ICING

This is generally a top icing. You can ice the top of any cake with this. For the inside of the cake, make half the quantity of chocolate butter icing given on page 144. Let the cake cool down completely before icing the cake. Cut into 2 pieces and sandwich the cake with chocolate butter cream. Prepare the stiff chocolate icing only when the cake is ready to be iced, otherwise the icing starts to set. The icing should be poured on the cake within a few minutes.

INGREDIENTS

**00 gm (¾ cup) cream, preferably cream available in tetra-packs like Amul cream
0 gm cooking chocolate or 2 dark slabs (40 gm each) of Amul, Nestle or
:adburys bournville chocolate - grated**

METHOD

1 Remove chocolate from the fridge and wait for a while till it is no longer very cold, but do not let it turn soft. Grate chocolate or chop into small pieces with a knife. Keep aside.

2 Heat the cream in a small heavy bottomed pan, on low heat, do not let the cream come to a boil.

3 Add grated chocolate and cook stirring continuously till chocolate melts and you get a smooth paste. Do not overcook. Actually when it is almost melted to a paste, remove from fire and stir gently till a smooth paste is ready. (Keeping the chocolate on fire for even a little longer can harden the chocolate!)

4 Immediately pour melted chocolate over the cake and tilt the cake to cover the top completely.

5 Arrange chocolate strawberries or cherries. Keep under refrigeration for 2-3 hours till icing sets.

CHOCOLATE STRAWBERRIES

Strawberries coated with stiff chocolate icing and chilled in the fridge to set. Use them to decorate cakes or desserts or enjoy them plain with a dollop of ice cream or just with coffee. You can use white chocolate too.

1 Wash strawberries. Prepare chocolate icing as given above. Hold the strawberry with the fork from the leaves and dip ¾ of the strawberry in prepared chocolate icing , leaving the top of the strawberry and leaves uncoated. Place on the greased aluminium foil. Keep in the fridge for the chocolate to set.

APPLE & DATE CAKE

A wonderful combination!

INGREDIENTS

Makes 8-10 slices

2 large apples - peeled, cored and chopped
½ cup butter - softened (75 gm)
1½ cups powdered sugar
2 eggs
2 tsp baking powder
2¼ cups flour (maida)
¾ cup walnuts - chopped
1¼ cups dates - stoned (seeds removed) and chopped

Cake browning too fast....

If the top of the cake or pie starts to brown too quickly, cover it with foil halfway through the cooking time to allow the inside of the cake to cook through without the top burning.

METHOD

1 Blend apples to a puree with 4 tbsp water in a mixer. Keep the puree aside.

2 Sift flour with baking powder. Keep aside.

3 Beat the butter and sugar in a pan nicely till light and fluffy with an electric hand mixer.

4 Add 1 egg and half of the sieved flour to the butter. Beat well. Add the remaining egg and flour. Beat well.

5 Add the apple puree. Mix.

6 Keeping aside 1 tbsp each of dates and walnuts for the top, add the rest of the walnuts and dates to the cake mixture. Mix well.

7 Grease and dust a big rectangular loaf tin or a round 9" cake tin. Spoon the mixture in the tin and bake in a preheated oven at 180°C/350°F, for about 1 hour or till done.

8 Cool for 5 minutes before removing the cake from the tin. Remove cake on a wire rack. Serve.

Preheating Oven...

Switch on the oven at the temperature you want to bake, the first thing when you start with the recipe. The oven should always be preheated for 10-15 minutes at the temperature stated in the recipe to get a well risen cake.

EGGLESS CAKE

Choose a large baking tin of about 10"-11" diameter for this cake. A smaller tin will give you a peaked cake and also it will take very long to get cooked from inside.

INGREDIENTS

erves 10

tin condensed milk (400 gm milk maid)
½ cups (250 ml) milk
½ cups (250 gm) flour (maida)
tbsp powdered sugar
cup (150 gm) butter - softened
tsp baking powder
tsp soda-bi-carb (mitha soda)
tsp vanilla essence, a drop of yellow colour, optional

METHOD

1   Grease a 10" round cake tin or a big square cake tin. Sprinkle 1 tbsp flour to dust the tin.
2   Preheat oven to 150°C/300°F.
3   Sieve flour, baking powder and soda-bi-carb together. Keep aside.
4   Beat butter, sugar and essence till butter turns fluffy.
5   Add milk and condensed milk. Beat well. (If the mixture looks curdled, beat over hot water.)
6   Add flour in 2-3 batches, mixing well after each addition. Add colour. Beat well for 4-5 minutes till the mixture is light and fluffy.
7   Transfer the cake mixture to the prepared tin. Level the mixture.
8   Place the tin on the wire rack. Bake at 150°C/300°F for 1 hour.
9   Insert a clean knife or a tooth pick in the centre of the cake. If it comes out clean, switch off the oven. Remove cake from oven after 5-10 minutes. Remove from tin after 5 minutes, by inverting on the wire rack.

EGGLESS CHOCOLATE CAKE

Follow the recipe given above, but add only 2 cups maida (plain flour) instead of 2½ cups. For the remaining ½ cup of maida, substitute it by adding ½ cup cocoa to the measured (2 cups) maida, to make the total amount to 2½ cups.

2 cups maida + ½ cup cocoa = 2½ cups

How do I keep the cake when it is ready?

Remove the cake on a wire rack after it is done. Let it cool to room temperature. Put it back in the baking tin and cover the tin with foil. Place a plate or lid on the aluminium foil. Keep outside the fridge. Only iced cakes are kept in the fridge.

TiP

All cakes make fantastic desserts when soaked with some orange juice, any cola drink or black coffee to make them soft and moist. Top with chocolate sauce and fruits. Serve with ice cream. A few toasted nuts on the ice cream taste even better!

WALNUT & RAISIN COOKIES

INGREDIENTS

Makes 20

¼ cup walnuts - crushed, ½ cup raisins (kishmish)
3 tbsp cornflour
1 cup flour (maida), ¾ tsp baking powder
1/3 cup (50 gm) butter - softened at room temp (do not heat butter)
½ cup + 2 tbsp powdered sugar (65 gm)
slightly less than ½ cup milk, approx., 1 tsp vanilla essence

METHOD

1 Beat sugar and butter till fluffy. Add essence. Beat well till mixed.

2 Sift flour, cornflour with baking powder. Mix walnuts and raisins to flour.

3 Add this flour to the butter-sugar mixture. Mix gently with a spoon.

4 Add enough milk to get a dropping consistency. The mixture should be thick or the cookies will spread on baking. Cover the back of a baking tray with aluminium foil and grease it with butter.

5 Put a spoonful of the batter on the prepared baking tray, 1" apart, to get irregular cookies. Press any kishmish on the top lightly. (It burns otherwise!)

6 Bake for 20-25 minutes in a preheated oven at 160°C/325°F or till golden and the bottom looks done. Cool cookies and store in an airtight box.

CASHEWNUT COOKIES

INGREDIENTS

Makes 16

100 gm (1 cup) maida (plain flour)
75 gm (½ cup) butter, margarine or vanaspati ghee -
softened at room temp (do not heat to soften)
50 grams (½ cup) powdered sugar
2 to 3 drops almond essence or 1 tsp vanilla essence
2 to 3 tbsp finely chopped cashewnuts or a few almonds
split into two pieces
seeds of 3-4 chhoti illaichi (green cardamoms) - crushed

METHOD

1 Preheat oven at 160°C.

2 Beat softened butter and sugar very well until light and creamy.

3 Add the essence and beat again.

4 Sift flour. Add the flour and mix gently to form a soft dough. (The dough feels as soft as a ball of boiled potatoes).

5 Form dough into small balls and roll into the chopped cashewnuts or arrange a piece of almond on top. Flatten slightly.

6 Prepare a baking tray by covering the backside of it with aluminium foil. Grease foil with some butter. Arrange the cookies 1" apart on the foil.

7 Sprinkle illaichi powder. Bake in a preheated oven for 15 to 20 minutes till they turn light golden and the base gets a little brown. Remove from the tray when slightly cold.

Are the cookies done?

The edges on the top turn golden and if you pick up the cookie, the underside is brownish and crisp. Cookies turn extra brown and burn very fast, so keep a watch when they start turning golden.

Desserts

Phirni

Your family will adore you for this simple, yet delicious Indian dessert. Set phirni in earthen containers to give a special flavour to the dessert.

INGREDIENTS

Serves 6

½ cups (750 gm) milk, ¼ cup basmati rice

¼ cup sugar plus 1 tbsp more, or to taste

almonds (badaam) - shredded

-6 green pistas (pistachio) - shredded

eeds of 2-3 chhoti illaichi (green cardamom) - powdered

drop kewra essence or 1 tsp ruh kewra

small silver leaves and a few rose petals - to decorate

METHOD

1. Soak rice of good quality for about an hour in a little water.

2. Drain rice and grind with 4-5 tbsp of water to a very fine and smooth paste. Mix rice paste with ½ cup milk and make it thinner. Keep aside.

3. Mix the rice paste with all the milk in a clean, heavy bottomed pan or kadhai. Cook on medium heat, stirring continuously and let it boil. Boil, stirring constantly for 2-3 minutes more to get a mixture of creamy consistency.

4. Add sugar and cardamom powder and mix well for a few seconds to dissolve the sugar.

5. Remove from fire and add ruh kewra or the essence and half of the shredded almonds and pistachios. Pour the mixture into 6 small bowls.

6. Decorate each bowl with a silver leaf, nuts and rose petals. Chill in the fridge till serving time.

Caution:

As soon as the phirni is done, pour immediately into the serving bowl/or individual small bowls (katoris) as it starts setting in the pan/kadhai. If you pour out the phirni later, it does not come out smooth with a velvety texture. It tastes a little lumpy.

Earthern Containers for phirni

Soak these mitti ki katori in water for 3-4 hours before use.

Vanilla Choco Surprise

INGREDIENTS

Serves 4-6

½ tin milk maid (condensed milk), 400 gm for full tin, at room
temperature
1½ tsp vanilla essence
200 gm cream
4 tsp gelatine
2-3 tbsp ready made chocolate sauce
¼ cup chopped fresh lichi or 1 tbsp kishmish

DECORATION
4-6 nice biscuits (sugar coated) or wafer sticks - optional
a few lichis - seed removed, a few cherries
some mint leaves - dipped in cold water

METHOD

1   Beat condensed milk in a deep bowl till light and creamy, for about 2-3 minutes, with an electric hand mixer. Keep aside.

2   Put ½ cup water in a sauce pan. Sprinkle gelatine on the water in the pan. Keep aside for 5 minutes to soften. Keep stirring on low heat for 2-3 minutes till gelatine dissolves.

3   Add the hot gelatine to the condensed milk and mix well. Add essence.

4   Add 1¼ cups water and mix gently till everything blends together. Keep in the freezer for ½ hour till slightly thick and half set.

5   Beat semi set dessert.

6   Add cream and beat well till well mixed. Add kishmish or chopped lichis and mix. Transfer to a serving dish.

7   Pour some chocolate sauce over the mixture in the dish. Mix gently to get a marble effect. Keep in the fridge for about 2-3 hours till set. (Do not put in the freezer.)

8   Insert a mint leaf and then a cherry in the lichi and arrange them on the dessert. Keep in the fridge till serving time.

9   To serve, insert the corner of the biscuit, such that only half of the biscuit shows as a diagonal piece of biscuit. Serve cold.

Gelatine turns rubber like...

If gelatine solution is added to a cold mixture, it starts to set immediately in small rubber like lumps instead of getting mixed with the mixture. So, be careful to see that the condensed milk is not cold when the gelatine is added to it.

Gajar ka Halwa

Carrot pudding.

INGREDIENTS

Serves 4

½ kg carrot - washed nicely and grated into long shreds
1 cup milk
¼ cup sugar
2-3 tbsp desi ghee
5-6 badam (almonds) - shredded
10-12 kishmish (raisins)
seeds of 3-4 chhoti illaichi (green cardamom) - powdered
100 gms khoya - grated

METHOD

1. Boil 1 cup milk in a clean kadhai.
2. Add grated carrots and cook uncovered, stirring occasionally, till milk dries.
3. Add badam and kishmish. Stir for 1 minute.
4. Add sugar. Cook till the mixture turns dry again.
5. Add ghee and stir fry for 10 minutes on low flame.
6. Add grated khoya. Mix well. Serve hot.

Glossary of Names/Terms

HINDI OR ENGLISH NAMES AS USED IN INDIA	ENGLISH NAMES AS USED IN USA/UK/ OTHER COUNTRIES
Achaar	Vegetables pickled in flavoured oil
Ajwain	Carom seeds
Aloo	Potatoes
Amchoor	Dry mango powder which makes a dish sour, 1 tsp of lemon juice can be substituted for ¼ tsp amchoor
Anjeer	Dry figs
Arhar dal	Yellow lentils
Atta	Whole wheat flour
Badaam	Almonds
Baingan	Eggplant, aubergine
Basmati rice	Fragrant Indian rice
Besan	Gram flour
Bharte waala baingan	Eggplant (aubergine) of big round variety
Bharwaan	Stuffed
Bhutta	Corn
Bhindi	Okra, ladys finger
Capsicum	Bell peppers
Chaat Masala	A spice blend (salty and sour blend)
Chaawal, Chawal	Rice
Chana dal/Chane ki dal	Gram lentils
Channe	Chickpeas
Chhole	Chickpeas
Chhoti Illaichi	Green cardamom
Chilli powder	Red chilli powder, Cayenne pepper
Cornflour	Cornstarch
Coriander, fresh	Cilantro
Cream	Heavy whipping cream
Curd	Yogurt
Dahi	Yogurt
Dal	Lentils
Dalchini	Cinnamon
Degi mirch	Red pepper powder which is not too hot, paprika can be substituted
Dhania powder	Ground coriander seeds
Dhania saboot	Coriander seeds
Essence	Extract
French beans	Green beans
Gajar	Carrots
Garam Masala	A blend of many fragrant spices. A tsp of garam masala may be substituted by crushing 1 clove, 2-3 peppercorns and seeds of ½ black cardamom
Ghee	Clarified butter
Gobhi	Cauliflower

Haldi	Turmeric powder
Hara Dhania	Cilantro/fresh or green coriander
Hari Gobhi	Broccoli
Hari Mirch	Green hot peppers, green chillies, serrano peppers
Hing	Asafoetida
Icing sugar	Confectioner's sugar
Illaichi	Cardamom
Imli	Tamarind
Jaiphal	Nutmeg
Javetri	Mace
Jeera Powder	Ground cumin seeds
Jeera	Cumin seeds
Kadhai/Karahi	Wok
Kaju	Cashewnuts
Kali dal	Whole black lentils
Kalonji	Nigella seeds (black oval seeds), some also call it onion seeds
Karela	Bitter gourd
Kasoori methi	Dry fenugreek leaves generally used as dried herb
Katori	Individual serving bowls resembling ramekins
Keema	Mince meat
Kesar	Saffron
Khoya	Full fat milk cooked till thick. In India such cakes are available. Ricotta can be used instead
Khumb	Mushrooms
Khus Khus	Poppy seeds
Kishmish	Raisins
Kofta	Balls made from minced vegetables or meat, fried and put in a curry/gravy/sauce.
Lauki	Squash
Macchi	Fish
Magaz	Melon seeds
Maida	All purpose flour, Plain flour
Makai, Makki	Corn
Makhan	Butter
Malai	Cream
Matar	Peas
Methi dana	Fenugreek seeds
Methi	Fenugreek greens
Mitha soda	Baking soda
Mooli	White, longish radish
Moong dhuli	Dried, skinned split green beans – a pulse
Moong phalli	Peanuts
Moti Illaichi	Black cardamom
Murg	Chicken
Mutton	Lamb
Nimbu	Lemon
Paalak/palak	Spinach

Paneer	Home made cheese made by curdling milk with vinegar or lemon juice. Fresh home made ricotta cheese can be substituted
Paraat	A shallow mixing bowl made of metal, usually for kneading dough
Parantha	Indian pan fried, flat bread
Patta Gobhi	Cabbage
Phalli	Green beans
Poodina, pudina	Mint
Powdered sugar	Castor sugar
Prawns	Shrimps
Pyaz, pyaaz	Onions
Raita	Spiced yogurt, with or without a vegetable
Rajmah	Kidney beans
Red Capsicum	Red bell peppers
Red chilli flakes	Red pepper flakes
Rind	Zest
Roti	Whole wheat, flat bread resembling tortillas
Saag	Cooked greens like spinach or mustard greens
Saboot Kali mirch	Peppercorns
Saboot Moong	Whole green moong beans – a pulse
Saboot Maanh	Whole black lentils
Sambhar	A South Indian preparation of yellow lentils resembling a thick soup/stew
Sarson ka saag	Cooked mustard greens
Saunf	Fennel
Seekh	Indian kabobs made of minced meat, generally barbecued or sometimes pan fried
Sela Chaawal	Parboiled rice, which when cooked is not sticky at all
Seviyaan	Vermicelli
Shimla Mirch	Green bell peppers
Soda bicarb	Baking soda
Spring Onions	Green onions, Scallions
Subzi	Cooked, dry vegetable dish
Suji	Semolina
Tadka	To temper a dish with spiced oil
Tamatar	Tomato
Tandoor	A clay oven, a conventional oven can be used instead
Tandoori masala	A spice blend, used for flavouring the marinade for barbecuing
Tawa	Griddle
Tej patta	Bay leaf
Tikka	Barbecued pieces of meat or vegetables
Til	Sesame seeds
Tinda	Courgettes, Round gourd
Toned Milk	Milk with 1% fat content
Tori	Zuchhini, the size is that of baby zucchini
White butter	Unsalted butter
Yellow Capsicum	Yellow bell peppers
Zeera	Cumin seeds

Understanding Restaurant Menus

If you've ever been too embarrassed to ask what an item on a menu is or have refrained from trying unfamiliar food at a restaurant because you don't know how to pronounce it, this section can help you. Terms used on restaurant menus can be confusing. Many are foreign words that describe a specific cuisine or dish; others describe ingredients or techniques. Here's a list of the most commonly used terms to guide you when you're eating out.

Aioli (ay-OH-le): Garlic mayonnaises, often served with fish, meat or vegetables; from southern France.

Alfredo (al-FRAY-doh): Rich Parmesan cheese sauce with butter and cream, usually served over fettuccine with fresh ground pepper; from Italy.

Au Gratin (oh-GRAH-tihn): Any dish topped with bread crumbs or cheese, then baked or broiled.

Au Lait (oh-LAY): Food or beverages served or prepared with milk.

Beef Tartare (tar-TAR): Finely chopped raw lean beef, sometimes served with capers, chopped parsley and onions.

Bordelaise (bor-dl-AYZ): Sauce made with red or white wine, beef stock or broth, shallots, parsley and herbs; usually served with beef.

Brioche (BREE-osh): A rich yeast bread made with butter and eggs; from France. It can be baked in a large round loaf or individual rolls; each usually has a "top-knot."

Brushcetta (brew-SHEH-tah): An appetizer of bread rubbed with garlic, drizzled with olive oil, heated and served warm.

Calamari (kal-a-MAHR-ee): Squid, known for chewy texture and mild flavor, often served as an appetizer.

Cappuccino (kap-poo-CHEE-no): Italian coffee topped with foam from steamed milk. Sometimes sprinkled with sweetened cocoa powder or cinnamon.

Carbonnara (kar-bo-NAH-rah): Dish of spaghetti, cream, eggs, Parmesan cheese and bacon.

Chiles Rellenos (CHEE-lehs reh-YEH-nohs): Mexican dish of cheese-stuffed chillies that have been dipped in batter and deep-fried.

Crostini (kro-STEE-nee): An appetizer of thin slices of toasted bread, brushed with olive oil. Can also be topped with cheese, tomatoes and herbs.

Flambe (flahm-BAY): Food presentation created by sprinkling dish with liquor and igniting just before serving.

Frittata (frih-TAH-ta): Egg dish with ingredients such as cheese and vegetables, cooked over low heat on top of the stove.

Gazpacho (gahz-PAH-cho): Spanish cold soup usually made from pureed tomatoes, peppers, onions, celery, cucumbers, olive oil, garlic, bread crumbs and vinegar.

Hollandaise (HOL-un-dayz): Creamy, buttery sauce with a touch of lemon, usually served with fish and eggs.

Lasagne: (la-ZAA-niya): Italian pasta which is in the form of sheets. These sheets are layered with filling, covered completely with a sauce and cheese. It is then baked till well set and firm.

Latte (LAH-tay): Espresso with lots of foamy steamed milk, usually served in a tall glass mug.

Marinara (Mah-ree-NAHR-a): Italian sauce for pasta and meat, made from tomatoes, onion, garlic and oregano.

Nicoise (nee-SWAHS): Dish that usually includes tomatoes, garlic, anchovies and black olives. A salad nicoise is made with green beans, onions, tuna, eggs and herbs.

Paella (pi-AY-yuh): Spanish dish of rice, saffron, seafood, meat, garlic, onion, peas, tomatoes and artichoke hearts, usually served in a wide, shallow pan.

Polenta (poh-LEN-ta): A cornmeal porridge from northern Italy. Made from cornmeal that is heated with water, then cooled and cut into squares, and fried or baked. It is often mixed with Parmesan cheese and butter and served with a sauce.

Prawn: Large shrimp; also the name of a seafood species that is more slender than shrimp and has longer legs.

Primavera (pree-ma-VEHR-ah): Dish that includes fresh vegetables; most well known is pasta primavera.

Quesidallas (ke-si-di-YAS): a Mexican snack which is made by sandwiching two tortillas with a cheesy filling between them. It is panfried and cut into pieces to serve.

Ragout (ra-GOO): French stew of meat, poultry or fish.

Risotto (ri-SAW-to): Italian dish prepared with arborio rice and hot stock or broth. Unlike other rice recipes, stock is added to rice gradually and cooked and stirred constantly to produce a creamy mixture.

Satay (say-TAY): Marinated cubes of meat, fish or poultry grilled on skewers and served with spicy peanut sauce, from Indonesia.

Scampi: Description of shrimp that have been split, brushed with butter and garlic, then broiled or grilled.

Strata: Dish layered with bread and mixtures of cheese, poultry or seafood topped with an egg-milk mixture, which puffs when baked.

Sushi (sue-SHEE): Japanese finger food consisting of slices of raw fish, rice, chopped vegetables, pickles and tofu all wrapped in sheets of seaweed.

Tetrazzini (the-trah-ZEE-nee): Italian dish of cooked spaghetti, Parmesan cheese, cream sauce and chicken. Turkey or tuna is sometimes substituted for chicken.

Tortilla (Tor-ti-Ya): The staple bread of Mexico. It is more or less like the Indian chappati. It can be made with plain flour or whole wheat flour or from corn meal.

INDEX